PRO-FOOTBALL
Brain Teasers

PRO-FOOTBALL

Brain Teasers

★ ★ ★ ★

Dom Forker
& Ted Forker

Sterling Publishing Co., Inc. New York

Dedicated to Nancy Forker
A Two-Way Threat:
Wife and Mother, and
Our Quarterback

Library of Congress Cataloging-in-Publication Data

Forker, Dom.
    Pro football brain teasers / Dom Forker & Ted Forker.
        p.   cm.
    Includes index.
    ISBN 0-8069-9452-5
    1. Football—United States—Miscellanea.   2. Football—Records—
United States. I. Forker, Ted. II. Title.
GV954.F67   1996
796.332'64'0973—dc20   96-9279
                                                        CIP

10 9 8 7 6 5 4 3 2 1

Published by Sterling Publishing Company, Inc.
387 Park Avenue South, New York, N.Y. 10016
© 1996 by Dom and Ted Forker
Distributed in Canada by Sterling Publishing
% Canadian Manda Group, One Atlantic Avenue, Suite 105
Toronto, Ontario, Canada M6K 3E7
Distributed in Great Britain and Europe by Cassell PLC
Wellington House, 125 Strand, London WC2R 0BB, England
Distributed in Australia by Capricorn Link (Australia) Pty Ltd.
P.O. Box 6651, Baulkham Hills, Business Centre, NSW 2153, Australia
Manufactured in the United States of America

Sterling ISBN 0-8069-9452-5

CONTENTS

INTRODUCTION

Professional football is a sport with a rich, colorful history. This is evident when you consider the many different record-setters of yesterday and today, whom you will meet in the following pages. But it is also reflected in the actual flesh-and-bone people who have played a focal point in the game. Not long ago, we contacted Sid Luckman, the quarterback who revolutionized the National Football League when head coach George Halas, through the influence of Clark Shaughnessy (the Stanford head coach), converted the Chicago Bears' offense from the single-wing to a T–formation in 1940.

Now retired and living in Miami, Florida, Luckman relived the 1940 championship game between the victorious Bears and the Washington Redskins, and also reflected upon his love for Halas, his old coach. He recalled that in 1940 the Bears lost their last regular-season game against the Redskins on a controversial play, 7–3. After the game, Washington owner George Preston Marshall criticized the Bears, calling them a bunch of crybabies. Halas responded by posting the clippings of Marshall's statements in the newspapers on the bulletin board in the Bears' dressing room.

"Marshall may think you're a bunch of crybabies," Halas told his players, "but I think you're the best bunch of football players and young men in America. Now it's up to you, in our next game, to prove it to yourselves, your families, and your countrymen."

Two weeks later, in one of the most significant and historic games in the history of the NFL, the Bears demolished the Redskins in the championship game, 73–0. This game was so significant because the new offensive concept ushered in the modern era of NFL history, and also because it was the first professional football championship contest to be broadcast nationally via radio. The Bears had used a T-formation offense with a man in motion all season. Opposing defenses responded by setting up a 5–4–2 (five linemen, four linebackers, and two defensive backs) alignment so that the secondary could slide with the man in motion. In the title matchup, Halas introduced a counter move without backfield blockers off the motion. The Washington defense couldn't stop the reverse attack. The Bears led 21–0 at the end of the first quarter, 28–0 at the half, 59–0 at the end of the third quarter, and 73–0 at the final whistle. Luckman threw for one touchdown and ran for another. The Redskins' game plan was in such disarray that the Bears ran three interceptions back for touchdowns.

The Redskins' fate was sealed in the second quarter when star quarterback Sammy Baugh was injured and had to leave the game. Someone asked Baugh after the contest what happened to Washington's game plan. "When you fall behind 21–0 at the end of the first quarter, your game plan goes out the window," Baugh retorted. "We were flat. They were so pumped up, I thought they would never come back to earth. But that's what happens when you run the other guys down and call them crybabies before a big game."

Luckman and Halas became a success story. From 1940 to 1943, the Bears played in the title game every year, winning three times and losing once, to Baugh's Redskins in 1942. But World War II broke up the Bears' juggernaut.

"Boy, we were good," assessed Luckman, who once threw a record seven touchdowns in one game. "And we were young, too. There's no telling how many championships we might have won." However, Luckman and some of his teammates served in World War II from 1944 to 1945, missing both football seasons. With the end of the war, Luckman and his teammates rejoined the Bears, and in 1946 regrouped to win one more championship, when they defeated the Giants in the championship game, 24–14. Several minutes into the fourth quarter, with the score tied at 14, Luckman shocked the Giants when he ran 19 years yards for a touchdown. A subsequent field goal iced the title for the Bears.

In his first five years, Luckman directed the Bears to four championships and one second-place finish. Despite his success, he found himself fighting to retain the top quarterback position on some talent-laden Chicago Bear teams. The

Bears' training camp in 1949 was a very competitive one. Halas had four of the most talented quarterbacks in the history of professional football vying for the starting job. Luckman was rated number one going into camp. The heir apparent for the job was Johnny Lujack, the 1947 Heisman Trophy Award winner from Notre Dame. While waiting to succeed Luckman, he became a standout as the secondary of the 1948–49 Bears. Also competing for a signal-calling spot were Bobby Layne out of the University of Texas and a quarterback/kicker out of the University of Kentucky, who went on to score a record 2,002 points in professional football. The name of this signal caller? George Blanda. All of them are in the Hall of Fame today except Lujack, who would be if he had not sustained severe back and shoulder injuries early in his career.

Halas sold Layne to the New York Titans before the season began. Layne eventually went to the Detroit Lions and led them to three championships in the 1950s. Halas knew in advance that he would regret the move. Later, he confided to Luckman that he would never again get rid of a top-quality quarterback.

"George knew what he had," Luckman recalled. "But he also knew that he could only play one of us. He should have retired me and kept Bobby [Layne]. He was a heck of a competitor. Lujack was the greatest college football player who ever lived. If he didn't get hurt, he might have been the greatest *pro football player* who ever lived."

With six games left in the 1949 season, Luckman sustained a hit to his neck and injured his thyroid gland. But Lujack rallied the Bears to six consecutive wins, passing for a record 468 yards and six touchdowns against the Chicago Cardinals in the season's finale. Though the Bears had a 9–3 record, the Los Angeles Rams, who were 8–2–2, were awarded the Western Division title, because they had defeated Chicago in both of their matchups.

It was time for Luckman to retire as quarterback, but he did not leave the Chicago Bears' organization. Instead, shortly thereafter, Luckman became a quarterback coach for them, a position he held for fifteen years.

According to Luckman, Halas was one of the stalwarts of the NFL. A renowned coach and also owner of the Bears, he was innovative, tough, and charismatic, and a tremendous leader and motivator. He won the first of his seven titles in 1921, at the age of 26, and his last championship in 1963, 42 years later, at the age of 68.

Halas was also a father figure to his players, keeping in touch with them over the years after their careers were over, no matter where they were. He and Luckman kept in touch right up until his death. In fact, Luckman visited Halas in the hospital nights before the legendary "Papa Bear" died. Soon after Sid left, Halas wrote a farewell note. It read: "My dear Sid, as I kissed you last night I realized my feelings toward you could be summed up in seven words: my pride in you has no bounds. Every time I complimented you, you would win another championship for us. You had a lust for the starlight that was never tarnished. God bless you and keep you, my son. I love you with all my heart."

The NFL's founding father passed away a few days later. "Every time I talk about this, I have tears in my eyes," Luckman concluded.

George Halas's name is just one of many that are cited in the quizzes that follow. Many of the other players mentioned have also played a pivotal role in pro football. By participating in these quizzes, you are taking advantage of an opportunity to explore a fascinating sport and an important part of Americana.

Dom Forker
Ted Forker
March 1, 1996

CHAPTER ONE

THE ABC'S OF PRO FOOTBALL

I. PRESENT-DAY PLAYERS

See how well you know today's players from A to Z. There is no letter X.

A._____An All-Pro quarterback, he has won 10 of his 11 postseason starts.

B._____He led the NFL with 4,555 passing yards in 1994.

C._____A running back, he caught 101 passes in 1995.

D._____This defensive end shares the NFL postseason single-game record with 3½ sacks.

E._____A quarterback, he has thrown 225 touchdown passes and amassed 41,706 yards over a 13-year career.

F._____In 1994, this running back rushed for 1,282 yards during his rookie season.

G._____His nickname is "Jumpy."

H._____A linebacker, he returned his first career interception for a touchdown in the 1995 Pro Bowl.

I._____A wide receiver, he has caught passes for a total of 7,093 yards over the past five seasons.

J._____He was the first fullback named to the NFC Pro Bowl squad.*

K._____This quarterback has thrown a record seven interceptions in the Super Bowl.

*The position of fullback was not added to the Pro Bowl roster until 1993.

L._____A defensive back, he returned three interceptions for touchdowns during his rookie season to tie Lem Barney's prior NFL record.

M._____A linebacker, he was selected by the Patriots as the fourth pick in the 1994 draft.

N._____A Pro Bowl tight end, he caught 62 passes for 705 yards and five touchdowns in 1995.

O._____In 1992, he returned an interception 103 yards for a touchdown to tie a league record.

P._____He led the NFL with 17½ sacks in 1995.

Q._____A wide receiver, he caught 56 passes for 654 yards and four touchdowns for the 1993 Cincinnati Bengals.

R._____He tied the NFL's postseason single-game record when he caught three touchdowns against the Oilers in 1993.

S._____He is the only person in history to play in both the World Series and the Super Bowl.

T._____A 49er, his 45-yard punt return has been the longest in Super Bowl play.

U._____This former Ohio State center was drafted by the Miami Dolphins in 1989 and currently plays for the New Orleans Saints.

V._____A fullback, he was dubbed "Touchdown Tommy" during his days at Stanford.

W._____He set a postseason single-game record when he scored five touchdowns against the New York Giants in 1993.

Y._____He set the Super Bowl single-game record with six touchdown passes.

Z._____A field goal kicker, he set a league mark when he was perfect in 17 tries in 1991.

II. Yesterday's Heroes

As in Section I, see how well you know yesterday's players from A to Z. Letters Q and X are omitted.

A._____A safety, he tied a league record when he picked off four passes for the Miami Dolphins in a 1973 game against the Pittsburgh Steelers.

B._____He caught 12 passes for 178 yards and a touchdown in the Baltimore Colts' overtime win over the Giants in the 1958 title game.

C._____A Detroit Lion, he returned eight punts for touchdowns, an NFL record.

D._____He has been the only person in pro-football history to serve as a scout, assistant coach, head coach, general manager, commissioner, and team owner.

E._____This defensive back scored the winning touchdown for the Eagles against the Giants in the "Miracle at the Meadowlands" on November 19, 1978.

F._____At the age of 19, this Bear lineman became the youngest starter ever to play in the league.

G._____He was nicknamed the "Galloping Ghost."

H._____He coached the Bears to seven league titles during 40 seasons on the sidelines.

I._____A Packer back, he teamed up with quarterback Don Hutson to score many touchdowns during the late 1930's and early 1940's.

J._____A defensive end, his specialty was the quarterback sack, a term he invented when he was a member of the "Fearsome Foursome."

K._____A 1,000-yard rusher in each of his first three seasons and a two-time punt return leader, he played for the Browns in the 1960's.

L._____His last-second touchdown pass for the Detroit Lions decided the 1953 title game against the Cleveland Browns, 17-16.

M._____A tight end for the Baltimore Colts, he was named to the All-NFL Team of the 1960's.

N._____A former star for the Cincinnati Reds in the 1919 World Series, he coached the Philadelphia Eagles to league titles in 1948 and '49.

O._____An Oakland Raider, he was named the AFL's all-time center.

P._____A fullback for the Dallas Cowboys in the 1960's, he gained 6,217 yards over an eight-year career, and participated in five Pro Bowls.

R._____He guided the Pittsburgh Steelers to four Super Bowl titles during his ownership.

S._____He was the first running back to run for 2,000 yards in a season.

T._____He threw four touchdown passes in his first pro game and then went on to hook up with receivers for 342 scores during a career with the Minnesota Vikings and the New York Giants.

U._____A Hall-of-Fame guard, he is presently the Executive Director of the NFL Players Association.

V._____This Eagle halfback was a four-time rushing champion.

W._____A former Cowboy safety, he shares the league record with nine career postseason interceptions.

Y._____A first pick for the Vikings in the 1968 draft, he was a perennial All-Pro offensive tackle out of the University of Southern California.

Z._____He quarterbacked the Seattle Seahawks from 1976 to 1984.

III. FAMOUS POSTSEASON GAMES AND PLAYERS

Match the player in the left-hand column with the postseason game he is famous or infamous for in the right-hand column.

1. Dwight Clark _____   A. "The Drive," 1986 AFC Championship Game

2. Drew Pearson _____   B. "Ice Bowl Block," 1967 NFL Championship Game

3. John Elway _____   C. "The Greatest Game?", 1958 NFL Championship Game

4. Frank Reich _____   D. "The Catch," 1981 NFC Championship Game

5. Jackie Smith _____   E. "The Guarantee," Super Bowl III (1968)

6. Jerry Kramer _____   F. "Hail Mary Touchdown," 1975 NFC Divisional Playoff

7. Ernest Byner _____   G. "The Dropped Pass," Super Bowl XIII (1978)

8. Franco Harris _____   H. "Greatest Comeback Ever," 1992 AFC First Round Playoff

9. Alan Ameche _____   I. "The Fumble," 1987 AFC Championship Game

10. Joe Namath _____   J. "The Immaculate Reception," 1972 AFC Divisional Playoff

Chapter Two
QUARTERBACKS

I. QUARTERBACKS WITH 4,000-YARD PASSING SEASONS

Compare each pair of quarterbacks listed below and determine which one of them had more 4,000-yard passing seasons. The answer chart in the back of the book lists the quarterback with more 4,000-yard passing seasons and the number of seasons involved.

1. _____ Dan Marino   or John Elway
2. _____ Warren Moon   or Steve Young
3. _____ Joe Montana   or Dan Fouts
4. _____ Joe Namath   or Roger Staubach
5. _____ Johnny Unitas or Phil Simms

II. QUARTERBACKS WITH 400-YARD PASSING GAMES

Compare each pair of quarterbacks listed below and determine which one of them had more 400-yard passing games. The answer chart in the back of the book lists the quarterback with more 400-yard passing games and the number of games involved.

1. _____ Dan Marino   or Joe Montana
2. _____ Sonny Jurgensen or Dan Fouts
3. _____ Boomer Esiason or Dave Krieg
4. _____ Steve Young   or Tommy Kramer
5. _____ Joe Namath   or Kenny Anderson

15

III. ALL-TIME CLUB-LEADING NFC QUARTERBACKS

Name the all-time club-leading quarterback in total passing yardage for each respective club. The teams are listed in alphabetical order in the left-hand column. The signal caller's total yardage is placed in parentheses.

1. Arizona Cardinals _____ (34,639)
2. Atlanta Falcons _____ (23,468)
3. Carolina Panthers _____ (2,717)
4. Chicago Bears _____ (14,686)
5. Dallas Cowboys _____ (22,700)
6. Detroit Lions _____ (15,710)
7. Green Bay Packers _____ (23,718)
8. Minnesota Vikings _____ (33,098)
9. New Orleans Saints _____ (21,734)
10. New York Giants _____ (33,462)
11. Philadelphia Eagles _____ (26,963)
12. St. Louis Rams _____ (23,758)
13. San Francisco 49ers _____ (35,124)
14. Tampa Bay Buccaneers _____ (14,820)
15. Washington Redskins _____ (25,206)

IV. ALL-TIME CLUB-LEADING AFC QUARTERBACKS

Name the all-time club-leading quarterback in total passing yardage for each respective club. The teams are listed in alphabetical order in the left-hand column. The signal caller's total yardage is placed in parentheses.

1. Buffalo Bills _____ (32,657)
2. Cincinnati Bengals _____ (32,838)

16

3. Cleveland Browns	_____	(23,713)
4. Denver Broncos	_____	(41,706)
5. Houston Oilers	_____	(33,685)
6. Indianapolis Colts	_____	(39,768)
7. Jacksonville Jaguars	_____	(2,168)
8. Kansas City Chiefs	_____	(28,507)
9. Miami Dolphins	_____	(48,841)*
10. New England Patriots	_____	(26,886)
11. New York Jets	_____	(27,057)
12. Oakland Raiders	_____	(19,078)
13. Pittsburgh Steelers	_____	(27,989)
14. San Diego Chargers	_____	(43,040)
15. Seattle Seahawks	_____	(26,132)

V. QUARTERBACKS AND THEIR ALMA MATERS

Match the quarterbacks in the left-hand column with the colleges for which they played in the right-hand column.

1. _____ Steve Young   A. Notre Dame

2. _____ Roger Staubach   B. Columbia

3. _____ Dan Marino   C. Maryland

4. _____ Danny White   D. Alabama

5. _____ Boomer Esiason   E. Southern Mississippi

6. _____ Bart Starr   F. UCLA

7. _____ Fran Tarkenton   G. Brigham Young

8. _____ Sammy Baugh   H. Pittsburgh

9. _____ Sonny Jurgensen I. Augustana

10. _____ Joe Montana   J. Arizona State

11. _____ Kenny Anderson K. Naval Academy

*NFL leader

12. _____ Troy Aikman	L. University of Miami
13. _____ Brett Favre	M. Duke
14. _____ Jim Kelly	N. Georgia
15. _____ Sid Luckman	O. Texas Christian

VI. TOUCHDOWN TANDEMS

Match the quarterbacks in the left-hand column with the receivers to whom they threw in the right-hand column.

1. _____ Joe Montana	A. Charley Hennigan
2. _____ Bobby Layne	B. Drew Pearson
3. _____ Joe Namath	C. Harold Carmichael
4. _____ Roger Staubach	D. Raymond Berry
5. _____ Otto Graham	E. Drew Hill
6. _____ George Blanda	F. Art Monk
7. _____ Terry Bradshaw	G. Mark Clayton
8. _____ Johnny Unitas	H. Dante Lavelli
9. _____ Dan Fouts	I. Don Maynard
10. _____ Warren Moon	J. Jerry Rice
11. _____ Jim Zorn	K. Charlie Joiner
12. _____ Troy Aikman	L. Sterling Sharpe
13. _____ Dan Marino	M. Lynn Swann
14. _____ Ken Stabler	N. Charley Taylor
15. _____ Ron Jaworski	O. Frank Gifford
16. _____ Joe Theismann	P. Fred Biletnikoff
17. _____ Charley Conerly	Q. Cloyce Box
18. _____ Sonny Jurgensen	R. Michael Irvin
19. _____ Jim Kelly	S. Steve Largent
20. _____ Brett Favre	T. Andre Reed

CHAPTER THREE

RUNNING BACKS

I. NFC TEAM ALL-TIME RUSHING LEADERS

Name the all-time leaders in total rushing yardage for each respective NFC club. The teams are listed in alphabetical order in the left-hand column. The running back's total yardage is placed in parentheses.

1. Arizona Cardinals _____ (7,999)
2. Atlanta Falcons _____ (6,631)
3. Carolina Panthers _____ (740)
4. Chicago Bears _____ (16,726)*
5. Dallas Cowboys _____ (12,036)
6. Detroit Lions _____ (10,172)
7. Green Bay Packers _____ (8,207)
8. Minnesota Vikings _____ (5,879)
9. New Orleans Saints _____ (4,267)
10. New York Giants _____ (5,989)
11. Philadelphia Eagles _____ (6,538)
12. St. Louis Rams _____ (7,245)
13. San Francisco 49ers _____ (7,344)
14. Tampa Bay Buccaneers _____ (5,957)
15. Washington Redskins _____ (7,472)

II. AFC TEAM ALL-TIME RUSHING LEADERS

Name the all-time AFC leaders in total rushing yardage for each respective club. The teams are listed in alphabetical

*NFL record

order in the left-hand column. The running back's total yardage is placed in parentheses.

 1. Buffalo Bills _____ (10,183)

 2. Cincinnati Bengals _____ (6,447)

 3. Cleveland Browns _____ (12,312)

 4. Denver Broncos _____ (6,323)

 5. Houston Oilers _____ (8,574)

 6. Indianapolis Colts _____ (5,487)

 7. Jacksonville Jaguars _____ (525)

 8. Kansas City Chiefs _____ (4,897)

 9. Miami Dolphins _____ (6,737)

10. New England Patriots _____ (5,453)

11. New York Jets _____ (8,074)

12. Oakland Raiders _____ (8,545)

13. Pittsburgh Steelers _____ (11,950)

14. San Diego Chargers _____ (4,963)

15. Seattle Seahawks _____ (6,705)

III. RUSHING TITLE LEADERS

Compare each pair of running backs listed below and determine which one of each pair has won more rushing titles. The answer chart in the back of the book lists the running back with more rushing titles, and the number of titles he has won.

1. _____ Walter Payton   or Jim Brown

2. _____ Gayle Sayers   or O. J. Simpson

3. _____ Eric Dickerson   or Marcus Allen

4. _____ Tony Dorsett   or Earl Campbell

5. _____ George Rogers or Franco Harris

IV. Running Backs and Their Records

Match the great running backs named here with the feats that they accomplished:

Earl Campbell   Marcus Allen
Walter Payton   Ottis Anderson
Eric Dickerson   Thurman Thomas
Tony Dorsett   Barry Sanders
O. J. Simpson   Franco Harris
Jim Brown   John Riggins
Emmitt Smith   Jim Taylor
Gayle Sayers

1._____This former Heisman Trophy winner set the league record with a 99-yard touchdown run.

2._____This powerful back rushed for 200 yards in a game four times in one season.

3._____In 1984, this explosive back rushed for 2,105 yards to set the league's single-season record.

4._____Identify the gridiron great who averaged a record 5.2 yards a carry for his career.

5._____This runner set a league record when he rushed for a touchdown in 13 consecutive games.

6._____Name the player who rushed for a record 25 touchdowns in one season.

7._____Identify the runner who carried the ball a record 3,838 times over a 13-year career.

8._____This Hall of Famer gained 200 or more yards in one game a record six times.

9._____Name the player who holds the record with 11 consecutive 100-yard games.

10._____Name the player who scored a record 22 touchdowns in his rookie season.

11._____Identify the double-threat runner who caught 13 passes against the Browns in a 1990 game to tie the league postseason record.

12._____This former Nittany Lion caught the "Immaculate Reception" pass in 1972.

13._____This runner led the league in rushing with 1,474 yards and scoring with 19 touchdowns in 1962.

14._____This back led the league with 1,833 yards rushing and a 5.7-yard per rush mark in 1994.

15._____This durable runner rushed for 1,000 yards in a season six times, but his best season was his first, when he totaled 1,605 yards on the ground in 1979.

V. RUNNING BACKS AND THEIR ALMA MATERS

Match the players listed in the left-hand column with the colleges for whom they played in the right-hand column.

1. _____ Larry Csonka   A. Pittsburgh

2. _____ Barry Sanders   B. Kansas

3. _____ Leroy Kelly   C. USC

4. _____ Tony Dorsett   D. Syracuse

5. _____ O. J. Simpson   E. Jackson State

6. _____ Ottis Anderson   F. Oklahoma State

7. _____ Gayle Sayers   G. Morgan State

8. _____ Walter Payton   H. Louisiana State

9. _____ Steve Van Buren   I. Illinois

10. _____ Franco Harris   J. University of Miami

11. _____ Emmitt Smith   K. Georgia

12. _____ Hugh McElhenny   L. Penn State

13. _____ Red Grange   M. Florida

14. _____ Ollie Matson   N. San Francisco

15. _____ Herschel Walker   O. Washington

Chapter Four

Receivers

I. NFC Team All-Time Receiving-Yardage Leaders

Name the all-time receiving-yardage leader for each respective NFC club. The teams are listed in alphabetical order in the left-hand column. The receiver's total yardage is placed in parentheses.

1. Arizona Cardinals _____ (8,497)
2. Atlanta Falcons _____ (5,635)
3. Carolina Panthers _____ (1,002)
4. Chicago Bears _____ (5,059)
5. Dallas Cowboys _____ (8,538)
6. Detroit Lions _____ (5,220)
7. Green Bay Packers _____ (9,656)
8. Minnesota Vikings _____ (7,636)
9. New Orleans Saints _____ (7,854)
10. New York Giants _____ (5,434)
11. Philadelphia Eagles _____ (8,978)
12. St. Louis Rams _____ (9,761)
13. San Francisco 49ers _____ (15,123)*
14. Tampa Bay Buccaneers _____ (5,018)
15. Washington Redskins _____ (12,028)

II. AFC Team All-Time Receiving-Yardage Leaders

Name the all-time receiving-yardage leader for each respective AFC club. The teams are listed in alphabetical order in

*NFL record

the left-hand column. The receiver's total yardage is placed in parentheses.

1. Buffalo Bills _____ (9,841)
2. Cincinnati Bengals _____ (7,101)
3. Cleveland Browns _____ (7,980)
4. Denver Broncos _____ (6,872)
5. Houston Oilers _____ (7,935)
6. Indianapolis Colts _____ (9,275)
7. Jacksonville Jaguars _____ (589)
8. Kansas City Chiefs _____ (7,306)
9. Miami Dolphins _____ (8,869)
10. New England Patriots _____ (10,352)
11. New York Jets _____ (11,732)
12. Oakland Raiders _____ (8,974)
13. Pittsburgh Steelers _____ (8,723)
14. San Diego Chargers _____ (9,585)
15. Seattle Seahawks _____ (13,089)

III. NFC TEAM ALL-TIME RECEPTION LEADERS

Name the all-time reception leaders for each respective NFC team. The teams are listed in alphabetical order in the left-hand column. The receiver's number of receptions is in parentheses.

1. Arizona Cardinals _____ (522)
2. Atlanta Falcons _____ (423)
3. Carolina Panthers _____ (66)
4. Chicago Bears _____ (492)
5. Dallas Cowboys _____ (527)
6. Detroit Lions _____ (336)

7. Green Bay Packers _____ (595)

8. Minnesota Vikings _____ (498)

9. New Orleans Saints _____ (532)

10. New York Giants _____ (395)

11. Philadelphia Eagles _____ (589)

12. St. Louis Rams _____ (593)

13. San Francisco 49ers _____ (942)

14. Tampa Bay Buccaneers _____ (430)

15. Washington Redskins _____ (888)

IV. AFC TEAM ALL-TIME RECEPTION LEADERS

Name the all-time reception leaders for each respective AFC team. The teams are listed in alphabetical order in the left-hand column. The receiver's number of receptions is in parentheses.

1. Buffalo Bills _____ (700)

2. Cincinnati Bengals _____ (417)

3. Cleveland Browns _____ (662)

4. Denver Broncos _____ (543)

5. Houston Oilers _____ (542)

6. Indianapolis Colts _____ (631)

7. Jacksonville Jaguars _____ (53)

8. Kansas City Chiefs _____ (416)

9. Miami Dolphins _____ (550)

10. New England Patriots _____ (534)

11. New York Jets _____ (627)

12. Oakland Raiders _____ (589)

13. Pittsburgh Steelers _____ (537)

14. San Diego Chargers _____ (586)

15. Seattle Seahawks _____ (819)

V. Receivers' Reunion

If the receivers who are listed in the left-hand column were to go back to their college reunions, where would these get-togethers take place? The colleges are listed in the right-hand column.

1. Art Monk
2. Jerry Rice
3. Steve Largent
4. James Lofton
5. Raymond Berry
6. Fred Biletnikoff
7. Chris Carter
8. Roy Green
9. Charley Taylor
10. Lynn Swann
11. Michael Irvin
12. Don Hutson
13. Andre Reed
14. Ahmad Rashad
15. Carl Pickens

A. University of Tulsa
B. University of Miami
C. Arizona State University
D. Kutztown University of Pennsylvania
E. University of Oregon
F. Stanford University
G. Syracuse University
H. University of Southern California
I. Mississippi Valley State
J. Ohio State
K. University of Alabama
L. University of Tennessee
M. Florida State
N. Henderson State
O. Southern Methodist University

VI. Royal Receivers

Compare each pair of receivers listed below and determine which one of them has more 1,000-yard seasons. The answer chart in the back of the book lists the receiver with more 1,000-yard seasons, and the number of seasons he has had.

26

1. _____ Jerry Rice   or James Lofton
2. _____ Steve Largent   or Charlie Joiner
3. _____ Sterling Sharpe   or Lance Alworth
4. _____ Michael Irvin   or Chris Carter
5. _____ Tommy McDonald or Art Powell

VII. TOUCHDOWN TWINS

Compare each pair of receivers below and determine which one of them has more touchdown receptions. The answer chart in the back of the book lists the receiver with more touchdown receptions, and the number of receptions he had.

1. _____ Jerry Rice   or Lance Alworth
2. _____ Fred Biletnikoff or Steve Largent
3. _____ Don Maynard   or Paul Warfield
4. _____Charlie Joiner   or Tommy McDonald
5. _____Art Powell   or Bobby Mitchell
6. _____ John Stallworth   or Harold Carmichael
7. _____ Charley Taylor   or Sonny Randle
8. _____ Harold Jackson   or Jimmy Orr
9. _____ Nat Moore   or Roy Green
10. _____ Cliff Branch   or Stanley Morgan
11. _____ Bob Hayes   or Raymond Berry
12. _____ Wesley Walker   or Mike Quick
13. _____ Dante Lavelli   or Gary Collins
14. _____ Drew Hill   or Art Monk
15. _____ Sterling Sharpe or Elroy Hirsch

CHAPTER FIVE

OFFENSIVE AND DEFENSIVE LINEMEN

I. LEADING THE WAY

Match the great offensive linemen in the left-hand column with the backs they have blocked for in the right-hand column.

1. Jim Ringo	_____	A.	John Riggins
2. Gene Hickerson	_____	B.	Tony Dorsett
3. Roosevelt Brown	_____	C.	O. J. Simpson
4. Nate Newton	_____	D.	Marion Motley
5. Larry Little	_____	E.	Mark Van Eeghen
6. Joe Jacoby	_____	F.	Barry Sanders
7. Mike Webster	_____	G.	Walter Payton
8. Herbert Scott	_____	H.	Frank Gifford
9. Reggie McKenzie	_____	I.	Emmitt Smith
10. Lomas Brown	_____	J.	Jim Taylor
11. Bill Willis	_____	K.	Chuck Foreman
12. Gene Upshaw	_____	L.	Larry Csonka
13. Ron Yary	_____	M.	Eric Dickerson
14. Jay Hilgenberg	_____	N.	Franco Harris
15. Jackie Slater	_____	O.	Jim Brown

II. IN THE TRENCHES

Answer the following questions as either True or False.

1._____The Bears' George Musso was the first player to achieve All-NFL status at two positions, guard and tackle.

2._____Hall-of-Fame guard Stan Jones is credited with being the first player to stress weight-lifting for football preparation.

3._____New England Patriot Hall-of-Fame guard John Hannah never played in a Super Bowl.

4._____Former Giant center Mel Hein is not in the Hall of Fame.

5._____Art Shell played guard for the Raiders.

6._____Cowboy Erik Williams was selected to the Pro Bowl in 1995.

7._____Charger and Raider Ron Mix had only two holding penalties in his 10-year career.

8._____The Dolphin offensive line of the 1970s was called "The Hogs."

9._____Packer guard Mike Michalske was the first guard to be enshrined in the Hall of Fame.

10._____Viking guard Randall McDaniel has been selected to seven consecutive Pro Bowls.

11._____Bart Oates, center for the 49ers, is a lawyer.

12._____Colt center Kirk Lowdermilk used to play for the Steelers.

13._____All-Pro Dolphin tackle Richmond Webb played college ball at the University of Texas.

14._____Bob St. Clair, former tackle for the 49ers, blocked 10 attempted field goals.

15._____Dolphin center Jim Langer played every offensive down in Miami's perfect 1972 season.

III. FAMOUS "FRONT FOURS"

Identify the lineman missing from the following great defensive "Front Fours":

1. Los Angeles Rams: Merlin Olsen, Rosey Grier, Deacon Jones, and _____

2. Pittsburgh Steelers: Joe Greene, Ernie Holmes, Dwight White, and _____

3. Minnesota Vikings: Carl Eller, Jim Marshall, Alan Page, and _____

4. Dallas Cowboys: Ed Jones, Randy White, Jethro Pugh, and _____

5. San Diego Chargers: Ron Nery, Earl Faison, Ernie Ladd, and _____

6. Detroit Lions: Darris McCord, Roger Brown, Sam Williams, and _____

7. Baltimore Colts: Gino Marchetti, Don Joyce, Big Daddy Lipscomb, and _____

8. New York Giants: Dick Modzelewski, Rosey Grier, Andy Robustelli, and _____

9. Kansas City Chiefs: Aaron Brown, Jerry Mays, Curley Culp, and _____

10. Chicago Bears: Dan Hampton, William Perry, Richard Dent, and _____

IV. Twenty Tough Tight Ends

Match the 20 tight ends listed below with their credentials that follow.

Dave Casper	Mark Bavaro
Mike Ditka	Todd Christensen
Kellen Winslow	Russ Francis
Jay Novacek	Ben Coates
Ozzie Newsome	Brent Jones
Shannon Sharpe	John Mackey
Riley Odoms	Jerry Smith
Billy Joe Dupree	Leon Hart
Bob Tucker	Jackie Smith
Pete Retzlaff	Jimmie Giles

1._____This former Colt amassed 331 receptions for 5,236 yards and 38 touchdowns. In 1992, he became the second tight end to enter the Hall of Fame.

2._____He is a former Plan B Free Agent who was named to the NFC Pro Bowl squad for the fifth consecutive season in 1995. He has also started for the Dallas Cowboys on three Super Bowl champs.

3._____A 1995 Hall of Fame enshrinee, this San Diego Charger is best remembered for his brilliant performance in a 1981 AFC playoff game, when he caught 13 passes for 166 yards and one touchdown, and blocked a potential game-winning field goal.

4._____This former Oakland and Los Angeles Raider caught 461 career passes and 41 touchdowns. He also rolled up three 1,000-yard receiving seasons and holds Oakland's single-season reception record with 95 in 1986.

5._____This Denver Bronco has already accumulated 313 receptions, 3,822 yards, and 21 touchdowns in six seasons. In a game against Buffalo in 1995, he caught 10 passes for 180 yards.

6._____A representative for the 49ers at the last four Pro Bowls, he had an exceptional year in 1994 when he accounted for 670 yards on 49 receptions and nine touchdowns.

7._____A renowned Bear and Cowboy, he had 427 receptions for 5,812 yards and 43 touchdowns in a Hall-of-Fame career.

8._____Primarily a St. Louis Cardinal, he amassed 480 receptions for 7,918 yards and 40 touchdowns. In 1994, he was the third tight end elected to the Hall of Fame.

9._____A Cleveland Brown, he racked up 7,980 yards on 662 career receptions. In 1981 and 1984, he had 1,000-yard seasons.

10._____This Giant had nine receptions for 101

yards and a touchdown in two Super Bowl appearances.

11._____A New England Patriot and San Francisco 49er, this All-Pro garnered 393 career receptions. He caught five passes for 60 yards in San Francisco's win in Super Bowl XIX.

12._____A Raider, he caught 378 career passes and scored 52 touchdowns. He holds Oakland's single-game record with 12 receptions.

13._____A former Notre Dame and Detroit Lion star, he had his best season in 1951, when he caught 35 passes for 544 yards and 12 touchdowns.

14._____A Giant and Viking, he had his best season in 1971, when he caught 57 balls for 791 yards. Overall, he snared 422 receptions.

15._____A Redskin from 1965 to 1977, he caught 421 passes and scored 60 touchdowns. He started for the Redskins in Super Bowl VII.

16._____This Eagle had 56 receptions in 1958 to tie Raymond Berry for the league lead. For his career, he had 452 receptions for 7,412 yards and 47 touchdowns.

17._____In 1994, he set the NFL single-season record for most receptions by a tight end when he caught 96 passes. Over the past three seasons, this Patriot has caught 233 passes for 2,748 yards and 21 touchdowns.

18._____A Bronco tight end from 1972 to 1983, he collected 396 receptions for 5,755 yards and 41 touchdowns, and he played in Super Bowl XII.

19._____In a career that spanned 13 years and four teams, he is best remembered as a Tampa Bay Buccaneer. He recorded 350 career receptions and 41 touchdowns, and still holds Tampa's single-game record with four touchdown catches.

20._____This Cowboy was selected to three Pro Bowls during his 11-year career. He amassed 267 receptions for 3,565 yards and 41 touchdowns, and caught six passes for 83 yards and a touchdown in two Super Bowl appearances.

CHAPTER SIX

LINEBACKERS

I. WHO'S WHO

Match the linebackers given below with the descriptions that follow.

Jack Lambert   Bill George
Ray Nitschke   Sam Huff
Junior Seau   Ken Norton Jr.
Lawrence Taylor   Joe Schmidt
Keena Turner   Jack Del Rio
Willie Lanier   Ken Harvey
Ted Hendricks   Mike Singletary
Derrick Thomas   Thomas "Hollywood" Henderson
Chuck Bednarik   Chris Speilman
Mike Curtis   Matt Millen

1._____Name the rookie "Man in the Middle" who anchored the Giants' defensive unit in their 1956 championship season.

2._____Identify the Giant linebacker who redefined the position by collecting 20½ sacks and the league's MVP Award in 1986.

3._____Can you recall the Detroit Lion middle linebacker who snagged 24 career interceptions, held the team's captain position for nine years, and was inducted into the Hall of Fame in 1973? He played with Detroit from 1953 to 1965.

4._____Do you remember the Chief linebacker, nicknamed "Contact," who picked off 27 career passes, and was the defensive star of Kansas City's Super Bowl IV upset of the Vikings?

5._____Name the "Steel Curtain's" middle linebacker who was a two-time NFL Defensive Player of the Year and a nine-time Pro Bowler.

6._____Identify the Colt, Packer, and Raider linebacker who blocked 25 field goals and extra points, intercepted 26 passes, played in 215 consecutive games, and was inducted into the Hall of Fame in 1990.

7._____Can you recall the Bear linebacker who made All-NFL eight times, appeared in eight consecutive Pro Bowls, and whose 14 years of service is the longest of any Bear player?

8._____Do you remember the former Baylor Bear and Chicago Bear who anchored Chicago's defense from 1981 to 1993, was selected to 10 Pro Bowls, and led the 1985 champions in Super Bowl XX?

9._____Name the Eagle middle linebacker-center who missed only three games in 14 years, and is infamous in New York for his crushing hit that knocked Frank Gifford "cold" in the 1960 playoffs.

10._____Identify the Packer middle linebacker who was the force behind Green Bay's defense in Super Bowls I and II. He was elected to the Hall of Fame in 1978.

11._____Can you recall the Chiefs' all-time sack leader, who is a seven-time Pro Bowler? He also holds the NFL's single-game sack record, with seven against the Seahawks in 1990.

12._____Do you remember the former USC Trojan, and current All-Pro Charger linebacker, who had eight games with 10 or more tackles in 1994, while leading his team to the Super Bowl?

13._____Name the former Lion linebacker who led Detroit in tackles for seven straight seasons, including a team-record 195 in 1994.

14._____Identify the former Cowboy and current 49er linebacker who has been the only player to perform on three consecutive winning teams in the Super Bowl.

15._____This former Raider, 49er, and Redskin linebacker won a Super Bowl title with each team during a career that spanned 12 seasons from 1980 to 1991.

16._____Do you recall the Colt, Seahawk, and Redskin "Mad Dog" linebacker from 1965 to 1978 who picked off 25 passes and anchored Baltimore's Super Bowl V championship team?

17._____Name the Cowboy linebacker who caused havoc on the field, but whose hard living ended his career prematurely. He frequently returned kickoffs.

18._____Identify the former Cowboy and Viking linebacker who has recorded five 100-tackle seasons in the last six years, and led Minnesota with 185 tackles, 67 of them solo, in 1994.

19._____Can you recall the former Cardinal and current Redskin linebacker whose 13½ sacks in 1994 led the NFC and earned him a Pro Bowl berth?

20._____Do you remember the former 49er linebacker who anchored the right side of the San Francisco defense that won four Super Bowl championships?

II. LINEBACKER TRUTHS OR FALSEHOODS

Answer the following questions as either True or False.

1._____Chuck Noll played as an offensive lineman and linebacker for the Cleveland Browns.

2._____Brian Bosworth made All-Pro with the Seattle Seahawks.

3._____Ken Norton Jr.'s father is a former heavyweight champion in boxing.

4._____Lawrence Taylor played his collegiate ball at North Carolina State.

5._____Jack Lambert body-slammed Cowboy safety Cliff Harris in Super Bowl X, after Harris had taunted Steeler kicker Roy Gerela for a missed field goal.

6._____Nick Buoniconti was the starting middle linebacker on the only undefeated team in NFL history.

7._____Lee Roy Jordan played middle line-backer for the Cowboys on two Super Bowl champion teams.

8._____Chuck Howley is the only linebacker to win the Super Bowl MVP Award.

9._____Cornelius Bennett led the AFC in sacks in 1994.

10._____When Carl Banks was at Michigan State, he worked as a grave digger during the summers.

11._____Clay Mathews has played more games than any other linebacker in league history.

12._____Lawrence Taylor led the NFL in sacks twice.

13._____Jessie Tuggle holds the NFL record for touchdowns off fumble recoveries.

14._____Jack Lambert played collegiate foot-ball at Michigan State.

15._____Jack Ham led all NFL linebackers in interceptions in 1972, with seven.

16._____Kevin Greene was a fifth-round draft choice by the Steelers in 1986.

17._____Patriot linebacker Willie McGinest has a wingspan of nearly seven feet.

18._____Bear fullback Bronco Nagurski also played tackle and linebacker.

19._____Harry Carson played one year with the Patriots.

20._____Renaldo Turnbull tied for the AFC lead with 13 sacks in 1993.

21._____Before going to the Carolina Panthers, Lamar Lathon played for the Chiefs.

22._____Former Bill linebacker Daryl Talley now plays for the St. Louis Rams.

23._____Dick Butkus played his collegiate ball for the University of Illinois.

24._____Redskin linebacker Ken Harvey never had an interception until he picked off a Jim Harbaugh pass in the 1995 Pro Bowl and returned it for a touchdown.

25._____Derrick Thomas has more sacks than any other linebacker.

CHAPTER SEVEN

DEFENSIVE BACKS

I. PASS THIEVES

Compare each pair of defensive backs listed below and determine which one has had more career interceptions. The answer chart in the back of the book lists the defensive back with more career interceptions, and the number of interceptions he had.

1._____Paul Krause or Dick "Night Train" Lane

2._____Emlen Tunnell or Dick LeBeau

3._____Ken Riley or Jim Patton

4._____Everson Walls or Ronnie Lott

5._____Mel Blount or Dave Brown

6._____Larry Wilson or Emmitt Thomas

7._____Mel Renfro or Johnny Robinson

8._____Bobby Dillon or Bobby Boyd

9._____Pat Fischer or Willie Brown

10._____Lem Barney or Jack Butler

II. POSTSEASON PICKS

Five of the ten players who are listed below have returned two or more interceptions for touchdowns in postseason play. Can you name them?

Lyle Blackwood	Paul Krause
Mel Blount	Jake Scott
Ronnie Lott	Everson Walls
Lester Hayes	Willie Brown
Darrell Green	Melvin Jenkins

1._____ 3._____ 5._____

2._____ 4._____

III. HAT TRICKS

Five of the 10 players who are listed below have returned three or more interceptions for touchdowns in a season. Can you identify them?

Ronnie Lott   Eric Allen
Everson Walls   Deion Sanders
Thom Darden   Herb Adderley
Rod Woodson   Emlen Tunnell
Mel Blount   Ken Houston

1._____

2._____

3._____

4._____

5._____

Chapter Eight

The Kicking Game

I. Famous Feet

Match the field goal kickers listed below with the famous feats that they performed.

Morten Andersen
Fuad Reveiz
Matt Bahr
Jim Bakken
Pat Leahy
Jim Martin
Lou Groza
Eddie Murray

Pat Summerall
Tom Dempsey
George Blanda
Mark Moseley
Jan Stenerud
Chris Boniol
Rich Karlis

1._____This kicker nailed a 49-yard field goal in a snow blizzard, with seconds remaining, to defeat the Cleveland Browns, 13–10, on the final day of the 1958 season, forcing a rematch playoff game the following week.

2._____Name the Giant kicker who connected on a 42-yard field goal as time ran out to beat the 49ers and advance New York to Super Bowl XXV.

3._____This legendary kicker led the league in field goals a record five times.

4._____Name the Viking kicker who made seven out of seven field goals in one game.

5._____This kicker has converted more 50-yard field goals than any other booter in league history.

6._____Name the former Lion who became the first kicker to convert two 50-yard field goals in one game.

7._____Identify the Cowboy kicker who converted five field goals, including the game-winner on the last play of Dallas's 21–20 victory over the Giants in 1995.

8._____This Cowboy kicker booted an over-time field goal in the last game of the 1993 season to defeat the Giants, 16–13, and earn Dallas the division title.

9._____Identify the kicker who booted an NFL-record 373 field goals.

10._____This 1970 Saint kicked a record 63-yard field goal.

11._____This quarterback-kicker scored an NFL-record 2,002 career points.

12._____Name the Jet kicker who scored 1,470 points in an 18-year career to place fourth on the all-time scoring list.

13._____This straight-on-style kicker was suc-cessful on 20 of 21 field goals for the 1982 Redskins.

14._____Identify the Viking kicker who made an NFL-record 31 consecutive field goals.

15._____This Cardinal attempted a record nine field goals in one 1967 game against Pittsburgh. He made seven, also a record.

II. POTENT PUNTERS

Answer each of the following questions with either a True or a False.

1._____Sammy Baugh's career punting aver-age of 45.1 yards an attempt is the best of any kicker with at least 250 attempts.

2._____Dave Jennings's 1,154 career punts are the most in league history.

3._____Jerrel Wilson, voted the AFL's all-time punter, had 12 punts blocked in his career.

4._____Ray Guy's punting average puts him among the top 20 all-time punters.

5._____Reggie Roby has never had a punt blocked.

6._____The Jets' Steve O'Neal's 98-yard punt is the longest in history.

7._____Ray Guy led the league in punting six times.

8._____The Eagles' John Teltschik once punted a record 15 times in one game.

9._____Norm Van Brocklin was not a punter.

10._____Bob Parsons of the Bears punted the ball a single-season-record 114 times in 1981.

11._____Danny White, not Ray Guy, led the NFL in punting in 1974.

12._____Rohn Stark led the AFC in punting average in 1995.

13._____Tommy Davis's career average of 44.68 yards per punt is the second all-time-best average.

14._____Reggie Roby led the NFC in punting in 1995.

15._____Harry Newsome of the Steelers had a record six punts blocked in one season.

16._____No punter has ever averaged 50 yards a punt for an entire season.

17._____Dave Jennings punted the ball 623 consecutive times without having one blocked.

18._____Herman Weaver of the Lions and the Seahawks and Harry Newsome of the Steelers and the Vikings had a career-record 14 punts blocked.

19._____Yale Lary of the Lions led the league in punting three times.

20._____Randall Cunningham's longest career punt is 80 yards.

CHAPTER NINE

FOOTBALL FIRSTS

I. FOOTBALL FIRSTS

See if you can pick the correct answers for the following 50 "Football Firsts."

1._____Who scored the first Super Bowl touchdown?
A. Elijah Pitts, B. Paul Hornung, C. Max McGee, or D. Mike Garrett

2._____Who was the first player that the Cowboys ever drafted?
A. Bob Lilly, B. Don Meredith, C. Lee Roy Jordan, or D. Danny White

3._____Who was the first Steeler to run for 200 yards in one game?
A. John Henry Johnson, B. John "Frenchy" Fuqua, C. Franco Harris, or D. Eric Pegram

4._____Who was the first quarterback to throw for 4,000 yards in a season?
A. Johnny Unitas, B. Sammy Baugh, C. Dan Marino, or D. Joe Namath

5._____Who was the first quarterback to throw for 400 yards in one game?
A. Sammy Baugh, B. Otto Graham, C. Sid Luckman, or D. Fran Tarkenton

6._____Who was the first player to rush for 2,000 yards in one season?
A. Eric Dickerson, B. O. J. Simpson, C. Ottis Anderson, or D. John Riggins

7._____Who was the first receiver to total 300 yards in one game?
A. Jim Benton, B. Jerry Rice, C. Charley Hennigan, or D. Steve Largent

43

8._____Who was the first Tampa Bay Buccaneer head coach?
A. Ray Perkins, B. John McKay, C. Leeman Bennett, or D. Bill Walsh

9._____Where was the first Super Bowl played?
A. Memorial Coliseum (Los Angeles), B. the Rose Bowl (Pasadena), C. the Orange Bowl (Miami), or D. Tulane Stadium (New Orleans)

10._____In what year did the AFC play the NFC for the first time in the Pro Bowl?
A. 1939, B. 1967, C. 1971, or D. 1985

11._____Who was the first player to register 20 or more sacks in a season?*
A. Lawrence Taylor, B. Reggie White, C. Charles Haley, or D. Mark Gastineau

12._____Who became the NFL's first black head coach in the modern era?
A. Ray Rhodes, B. Art Shell, C. Dennis Green, or D. Jim Brown

13._____Who defeated the Giants, 23–17, in the first sudden-death overtime game in an NFL championship contest?
A. Colts, B. Browns, C. Packers, or D. Lions

14._____Who became the first player in league history to rush for 1,000 yards in consecutive seasons?
A. Jim Brown, B. Joe Perry, C. Gale Sayers, or D. Alan Ameche

15._____Who was the first quarterback to throw 30 touchdowns in one season?
A. Dan Marino, B. Bob Waterfield, C. John Brodie, or D. Johnny Unitas

16._____Which kicker became the first one to boot 20 field goals in one season?

*Sacks have been recorded only since 1982.

A. Lou Groza, B. Pat Summerall, C. Bob Waterfield, or D. Jan Stenerud

17. _____Who became the first NFL player to score 20 touchdowns in one season?
A. Jim Brown, B. Duane Thomas, C. Lenny Moore, or D. Gale Sayers

18. _____Who was the first player picked in the 1969 draft?
A. O. J. Simpson, B. Terry Bradshaw, C. Joe Greene, or D. John Elway

19. _____Who won the very first Monday Night Football Game?
A. Jets, B. Cowboys, C. Raiders, or D. Browns

20. _____Which team was the first one to score 400 points in a season?
A. 1950 Rams, B. 1949 Eagles, C. 1984 Dolphins, or D. 1987 49ers

21. _____Who was the first and only NFL rushing champ to play on a Super Bowl winner in the same season?
A. Walter Payton, B. Emmitt Smith, C. O. J. Simpson, or D. Tony Dorsett

22. _____Who was the first coach to lead his team to three Super Bowl titles?
A. Bill Walsh, B. Chuck Noll, C. Joe Gibbs, or D. Vince Lombardi

23. _____Who was the first NFL player to score 100 career touchdowns?
A. Jerry Rice, B. Don Hutson, C. Lenny Moore, or D. Jim Brown

24. _____Who was the first coach to perfect the shotgun offense?
A. Bill Walsh, B. Vince Lombardi, C. Mike Ditka, or D. Tom Landry

25. _____Which of the following coaches led the

Steelers to their first winning season?
A. Walt Kiesling, B. Joe Bach, C. Chuck Noll, or
D. Johnny Michelosen

26._____Who was the first recipient of the Jim
Thorpe Trophy, in 1955, awarded to the NFL's most
valuable player?
A. Sid Luckman, B. Bobby Layne, C. Mike Ditka, or
D. Harlon Hill

27._____Who was the first black quarterback to
play in the NFL?
A. Doug Williams, B. Willie Thrower, C. Vince Evans, or
D. Joe Gilliam

28._____What team did the Steelers defeat to
win their first Super Bowl title?
A. Vikings, B. Cowboys, C. Los Angeles Rams, or D.
Redskins

29._____Who did the Cowboys select with the
first pick of the 1974 NFL draft?
A. Steve Deberg, B. Ed "Too Tall" Jones, C. Randy White,
or D. Danny White

30._____Who was the first original Cowboy in-
ducted into the Pro Football Hall of Fame?
A. Bob Lilly, B. Mel Renfro, C. Roger Staubach, or
D. Thomas Henderson

31._____Who was the Seahawks' first head
coach?
A. Mike McCormack, B. Chuck Knox, C. Jack Patera, or
D. Dennis Erickson

32._____Who was the first quarterback to
throw 40 touchdown passes in one season?
A. Dan Marino, B. Joe Montana, C. Jim Kelly, or D. Earl
Morrall

33._____Who was the Heisman Trophy Award
winner whom the Eagles picked as the first player ever
selected in the draft, in 1936?

A. Tom Harmon, B. Sam Francis, C. Jay Berwanger, or D. Angelo Bertelli

34._____Who did the 49ers select with their first pick in the 1951 draft?
A. John Brodie, B. Earl Morrall, C. Y. A. Tittle, or D. Hugh McElhenny

35._____Name the Bronco receiver who was the first Denver receiver to make the Pro Bowl since John Elway became quarterback?
A. Anthony Miller, B. Mark Jackson, C. Vance Johnson, or D. Steve Watson

36._____Who was the first receiver to gain 1,000 yards via the air in one season?
A. Jerry Rice, B. Don Hutson, C. Steve Largent, or D. Al Toon

37._____Who was the first player to lead the NFL in sacks in consecutive seasons?
A. Reggie White, B. Mark Gastineau, C. Fred Dean, or D. Richard Dent

38._____Who in 1941 was named the first commissioner of the NFL?
A. Bert Bell, B. Pete Rozelle, C. Elmer Layden, or D. Paul Tagliabue

39._____What team was the first wild-card club to make it to the Super Bowl?
A. Cowboys, B. Raiders, C. Dolphins, or D. Lions

40._____Who was the first coach to win both an NFL and an AFL title?
A. Tom Landry, B. Vince Lombardi, C. Weeb Ewbank, or D. Hank Stram

41._____Which NFL team was the first club to play its home games in a domed stadium?
A. Vikings, B. Oilers, C. Lions, or D. Saints

42._____Who was the first soccer-style kicker to play in the NFL?

A. Pete Gogolak, B. Jan Stenerud, C. Lou Groza, or D. Garo Yepremian

43._____Name the year when NFL players' names appeared on the back of their jerseys for the first time.
A. 1985, B. 1970, C. 1960, or D. 1975

44._____Who did the Carolina Panthers defeat for their first victory?
A. 49ers, B. Jets, C. Raiders, or D. Bengals

45._____Who did the Jacksonville Jaguars defeat for their first victory?
A. Oilers, B. Browns, C. Cowboys, or D. Chiefs

46._____Who was the first Cowboy to record 100 receptions in a season?
A. Drew Pearson, B. Michael Irvin, C. Lance Alworth, or D. Tony Hill

47._____Who was the first player to intercept four passes in one game?
A. Don Sandifer, B. Russ Craft, C. Sammy Baugh, or D. Dick Anderson

48._____Who was the first full-time offensive lineman inducted into the Hall of Fame?
A. Art Shell, B. Jim Parker, C. Jim Otto, or D. Jim Ringo

49._____Who was the first player who was recognized for spiking a football after scoring a touchdown?
A. Michael Irvin, B. Billy "White Shoes" Johnson, C. Jim Brown, or D. Homer Jones

50._____Who was the first player to kick five field goals in one game?
A. Tony Zendejas, B. Lou Groza, C. Bob Waterfield, or D. George Blanda

II. RECORD SETTERS

Match each player in the left-hand column with the record he set in the right-hand column.

1. ____ Norm Van Brocklin	A.	Has rushed for five career Super-Bowl touchdowns
2. ____ Don Hutson	B.	Played 26 seasons
3. ____ Joe Montana	C.	Scored 176 points in one season
4. ____ Eric Dickerson	D.	18 consecutive games scoring a touchdown
5. ____ Dan Marino	E.	Completed 22 consecutive passes
6. ____ Lenny Moore	F.	Led league in passing six times
7. ____ Paul Hornung	G.	14 interceptions in one season
8. ____ Derrick Thomas	H.	Threw 48 touchdowns in one season
9. ____ Emmitt Smith	I.	Rushed for 2,105 yards in one season
10. ____ Mark Gastineau	J.	Led league in pass receiving eight times
11. ____ Jerry Rice	K.	Threw for 554 yards in one game
12. ____ Charley Hennigan	L.	22 sacks in one season
13. ____ Dick Lane	M.	Seven sacks in a game
14. ____ Marcus Allen	N.	146 touchdown receptions
15. ____ Ken Houston	O.	336 yards pass receiving in a game
16. ____ George Blanda	P.	Three 200-yard pass-receiving games in one season
17. ____ Herman Moore	Q.	Sacked 72 times in one season

49

18. _____ Willie Anderson   R. 74-yard Super Bowl touchdown run

19. _____ Sammy Baugh   S. Returned nine career interceptions for touchdowns

20. _____ Randall Cunningham   T. 123 receptions in one season

CHAPTER TEN

COACHES

I. NFL HEAD COACHES

Answer the following 30 questions as either True or False.

1._____Paul Brown and Blanton Collier are the only Cleveland Brown coaches to win at least 50 games.

2._____Paul Brown is the only Bengal coach to win at least 50 games.

3._____Forrest Gregg has coached the Browns, the Bengals, and the Packers.

4._____Hall-of-Fame tackle Glen "Turk" Edwards coached the Redskins.

5._____Chuck Knox had a winning record as coach of the Bills.

6._____Bud Grant was the first coach of the Vikings.

7._____Bill Parcells is the Giants' all-time winning coach.

8._____Barry Switzer is the only Cowboy coach to win his first game.

9._____George Seifert has the best winning percentage of any coach in the history of the NFL.

10._____Marty Schottenheimer has the highest winning percentage of any Kansas City Chief head coach.

11._____Chuch Noll is the only coach to lead his team to four consecutive Super Bowls.

12._____Bill Parcells played linebacker for the Lions.

13._____Eagle coach Ray Rhodes was an assistant coach on all five 49er Super Bowl–champion teams.

14._____Don Shula's teams, the Colts and Dol-

51

phins, apeared in six Super Bowls and won two of them.

15._____Marv Levy has been the head coach of just one team, the Bills.

16._____Vince Lombardi won more games than any other Packer coach.

17._____Jim Mora has been the only Saint coach with a winning record.

18._____Joe Kuharich had a winning record as coach of the Eagles.

19._____Bill Cowher was a backup linebacker with the Steelers and the Browns.

20._____Mike Holmgren was a backup quarterback on the Jets' Super Bowl–champion team.

21._____George Allen had a better career-winning percentage than Mike Ditka.

22._____Tom Landry's 20 postseason victories are the most in league history.

23._____George Halas's 40 seasons on the sidelines with the Bears are the most in league history.

24._____John Madden has more career victories than Marv Levy.

25._____Dan Reeves was a running back with the Cowboys.

26._____Dan Reeves is the only coach to lead the Broncos to the Super Bowl.

27._____Weeb Ewbank is not in the Pro Football Hall of Fame.

28._____Sid Gillman was the first coach to win division titles in both the NFL and the AFL.

29._____Johnny Robinson coached the Rams in Super Bowl XIV.

30._____Wayne Fontes is not the Lions' all-time winning coach.

II. Who Succeeded Whom?

Take the 10 coaches who are listed below and match them up
with the famous coaches whom they replaced.

Les Steckel	Tom Flores
Paul Wiggin	Don Shula
Jimmy Johnson	Phil Bengtson
Blanton Collier	Jim Lee Howell
Bill Cowher	Jerry Burns

1. Paul Brown (Browns) _____
2. Weeb Ewbank (Colts) _____
3. Tom Landry (Cowboys) _____
4. Vince Lombardi (Packers) _____
5. Hank Stram (Chiefs) _____
6. Steve Owen (Giants) _____
7. John Madden (Raiders) _____
8. Bud Grant (Vikings, first time) _____
9. Bud Grant (Vikings, second time) _____
10. Chuck Noll (Steelers) _____

III. Super Bowl Winning Coaches

The 15 head coaches who are listed below have all guided
their teams to Super Bowl titles. One coach has won four
titles, two have copped three, seven have walked away with
two, and six have garnered one. Try to match each coach
with the number of titles he has won. The number of titles
are in parentheses.

One coach was omitted from the list. He led the Baltimore
Colts to victory over the Cowboys in Super Bowl V. Do you
know who he is? (Write his name in the space for number 16.)

Chuck Noll	Tom Landry	Vince Lombardi
Bill Parcells	Mike Ditka	Tom Flores
Don Shula	Weeb Ewbank	Joe Gibbs
John Madden	Barry Switzer	Bill Walsh
Hank Stram	Jimmy Johnson	George Seifert

1. _____	(4)	9. _____	(2)
2. _____	(3)	10. _____	(2)
3. _____	(3)	11. _____	(1)
4. _____	(2)	12. _____	(1)
5. _____	(2)	13. _____	(1)
6. _____	(2)	14. _____	(1)
7. _____	(2)	15. _____	(1)
8. _____	(2)	16. _____	(1)

IV. ALL-TIME COACHING WINS

Rank the following coaches in the order of their all-time regular-season wins.

I.

George Halas   1. _____ (328)
Chuck Noll   2. _____ (318)
Don Shula   3. _____ (250)
Tom Landry   4. _____ (226)
Curly Lambeau   5. _____ (193)

II.

Paul Brown   1. _____ (186)
Hank Stram   2. _____ (166)
Steve Owen   3. _____ (158)
Chuck Knox   4. _____ (151)
Bud Grant   5. _____ (131)

III.

George Allen   1. _____ (130)
John Madden   2. _____ (122)
Weeb Ewbank   3. _____ (116)
Sid Gillman   4. _____ (106)
Mike Ditka   5. _____ (103)

CHAPTER ELEVEN

NFL CHAMPIONS

I. NFL CHAMPIONS

The following questions are a chronology of NFL championship games from 1933 through 1965. How well do you know the NFL champions?

1._____Who led the Bears to a 23–21 win over the New York Giants in the 1933 NFL title game?
A. Bronko Nagurski, B. Johnny Lujack, C. Sid Luckman, or D. Vince Evans

2._____In 1934, the Bears were defeated in the title game, 30–13. Who beat them?
A. New York Giants, B. Detroit Lions, C. Green Bay Packers, or D. Boston Redskins

3._____In 1935, the Giants lost the championship game again, 26–7. Who defeated them?
A. Green Bay Packers, B. Detroit Lions, C. Chicago Bears, or D. Chicago Cardinals

4._____In 1936, the Green Bay Packers defeated the Boston Redskins, 21–6. What future Hall-of-Fame receiver opened the scoring with a 43-yard touchdown reception?
A. Al Rose, B. Bob Tenner, C. Dom Vairo, or D. Don Hutson

5._____In 1937, a slinging rookie passer completed 17 of 34 passes and two touchdowns to lead the Washington Redskins to a 28–21 triumph over the Chicago Bears. Who was that rookie?
A. Cliff Battles, B. Dixie Howell, C. Sammy Baugh, or D. Sonny Jurgensen

6._____The 1938 title game was between New York and Green Bay. Which Giant caught the decisive touchdown pass in their 23–17 victory?

A. Frank Gifford, B. Hank Soar, C. Jim Lee Howell, or D. Hap Barnard

7._____In 1939, the Packers dominated the Giants and beat them, 27–0, while holding their opponent to only nine first downs. Who was Green Bay's coach?
A. Vince Lombardi, B. Lisle Blackbourn, C. Earl "Curly" Lambeau, or D. Forrest Gregg

8._____Which Bear quarterback led his club to a 73–0 annihilation of the Redskins in the 1940 title game?
A. Johnny Lujack, B. Sid Luckman, C. Bobby Douglass, or D. Jim McMahon

9._____Playing exactly two weeks after the attack on Pearl Harbor, the Chicago Bears defended their title, beating New York, 37–9, for the 1941 NFL championship. Who was New York's coach?
A. Steve Owen, B. Jim Lee Howell, C. Allie Sherman, or D. Alex Webster

10._____The Redskins got revenge for 1940, when they defeated Chicago, 14–6, in the 1942 championship game. Who coached Washington to victory?
A. Ray Flaherty, B. George Allen, C. Joe Kuharich, or D. Otto Graham

11._____Which Bear quarterback threw five touchdown passes in the 1943 title game?
A. Sid Luckman, B. Johnny Lujack, C. George Blanda, or D. Bill Wade

12._____Name the Packer fullback who scored two touchdowns in the 1944 championship game?
A. Paul Hornung, B. Ted Fritsch, C. Joe Laws, or D. Edgar Bennett

13._____What quarterback led the Cleveland Rams over the Washington Redskins in the 1945 championship game?
A. Jim Hardy, B. Albie Reisz, C. Bob Waterfield, or D. Pat Haden

14._____Identify the New York back who was suspended by Commissioner Bert Bell for not reporting an attempted bribe before the 1946 NFL title game.
A. Frank Gifford, B. Joe Morris, C. Merle Hapes, or D. Gordon Paschka

15._____Which Chicago Cardinal Hall of Famer rushed 44 yards for one touchdown and returned a punt 75 yards for another score in the Cardinals' 1947 NFL championship-game win over Philadelphia?
A. Larry Centers, B. Dan Dierdorf, C. Charlie Trippi, or D. Marshall Goldberg

16._____Who scored the only touchdown in the 1948 championship game as the Eagles defeated the Chicago Cardinals in a heavy snowstorm, 7–0?
A. Steve Van Buren, B. Jack Ferrante, C. Russ Craft, or D. Pat McHugh

17._____Which Philadelphia quarterback completed five of nine passes for 68 yards and one touchdown in the Eagles' 1949 title-game win over Los Angeles?
A. Bill Mackrides, B. Norm Van Brocklin, C. Tommy Thompson, or D. Ron Jaworski

18._____Which Cleveland receiver caught two of Otto Graham's four touchdown passes in the Browns' 1950 championship-game win over Los Angeles?
A. Marion Motley, B. Dante Lavelli, C. Dub Jones, or D. Paul Warfield

19._____Which Los Angeles Ram caught a 73-yard fourth-quarter touchdown pass to down the Browns in the 1951 title game?
A. Elroy "Crazy Legs" Hirsch, B. Dan Towler, C. Henry Ellard, or D. Tom Fears

20._____Which Lion ran for 97 yards, including a 67-yard touchdown, in Detroit's 1952 win over Cleveland?
A. Bob Hoernschemeyer, B. Bobby Layne, C. Billy Simms, or D. Doak Walker

21._____Which Cleveland quarterback completed only two of fifteen passes in the Browns' 17–16 loss to Detroit in 1953?
A. Bob Waterfield, B. Otto Graham, C. Brian Sipe, or D. Bernie Kosar

22._____The Browns snapped their title-game losing streak by beating Detroit, 56–10, in 1954. Who caught five passes for 94 yards and two scores?
A. Ray Renfro, B. Dante Lavelli, C. Mo Bassett, or D. Michael Jackson

23._____In 1955, Cleveland sent Otto Graham out a winner, defeating Los Angeles, 38–14. Who was the Rams' rookie head coach?
A. Hamp Pool, B. Bob Waterfield, C. George Allen, or D. Sid Gillman

24._____Who was the former Giant (turned defensive coach) who earned a reputation guiding a solid New York defense to the 1956 title?
A. Bill Arnsparger, B. Tom Landry, C. Emlen Tunnell, or D. Alex Webster

25._____Which Lion quarterback filled in for the injured Bobby Layne and threw four touchdown passes to lead Detroit over Cleveland, 59–14, in 1957?
A. Tobin Rote, B. Eric Hipple, C. Tom Dublinsky, or D. Milt Plum

26._____Arguably the greatest game ever, the 1958 title contest was decided in overtime when what Colt back sliced into the end zone at Yankee Stadium?
A. Lenny Moore, B. Raymond Berry, C. Jim Mutscheller, or D. Alan Ameche

27._____Which Baltimore quarterback threw for two touchdowns and ran for another in the Colts' 31–16 win over New York in 1959?
A. George Shaw, B. Johnny Unitas, C. Bert Jones, or D. Art Schlichter

28._____In the 1960 championship game Philadelphia defeated Green Bay, 17–13. Who was the first and only coach to beat Vince Lombardi in a title game?
A. Hugh Devore, B. Lawrence "Buck" Shaw, C. Joe Kuharich, or D. Dick Vermeil

29._____Which Packer rushed for 89 yards and one touchdown, caught four passes for 80 yards, and kicked three field goals in Green Bay's 37–0 win over the Giants in 1961?
A. Paul Hornung, B. Jim Taylor, C. Tommy Moore, or D. Sterling Sharpe

30._____In 1962, Green Bay defeated New York, 16–7. Which Packer rushed for the game's only touchdown?
A. Jim Taylor, B. Paul Hornung, C. Bart Starr, or D. Eddie Lee Ivory

31._____In 1963, the Giants led the Bears, 7–0, when a Y. A. Tittle pass bounced off a wide-open Giant in the end zone. Chicago went on to win, 14–10. Who was that usually sure-handed New York receiver?
A. Frank Gifford, B. Hugh McElhenny, C. Mike Sherrard, or D. Del Shofner

32._____In the 1964 title game, which Cleveland receiver caught three touchdowns in the Browns' 27–0 whitewashing of the Colts?
A. Paul Warfield, B. Leroy Kelly, C. Gary Collins, or D. Andre Rison

33._____In 1965, Vince Lombardi's Packers defeated the Browns, 23–12. Who was Cleveland's head coach?
A. Paul Brown, B. Sam Rutigliano, C. Blanton Collier, or D. Forrest Gregg

Chapter Twelve
The Super Bowl

I. Super Bowl Chronology

There have been 30 Super Bowls. Super Bowl Sunday began on January 15, 1967, and has been continued every year since. We're going to give you one question in sequence for each Super Bowl, to test your knowledge of all the Super Bowls.

1._____Who scored two touchdowns in the first Super Bowl?

2._____Name the Packer who booted four field goals in Super Bowl II.

3._____Which Jet running back rushed for 121 yards and a touchdown in Super Bowl III?

4._____Who was the Viking starting quarterback in Super Bowl IV?

5._____Who kicked the only game-winning field goal in Super Bowl play, which occurred in Super Bowl V?

6._____Name the Cowboy back who rushed for 95 yards and a touchdown in Dallas' victory over Miami in Super Bowl VI?

7._____Name the kicker whose misplayed field-goal attempt and subsequent fumble was returned for the Redskins' only touchdown in Super Bowl VII.

8._____Which Miami running back rushed for 145 yards and a touchdown in Super Bowl VIII?

9._____Who was the Steeler defensive end whose sack of Fran Tarkenton for a safety was the only score of the first half in Super Bowl IX?

10._____Who caught four passes for 161 yards and a touchdown in the Steelers' first title-game win over the Cowboys in Super Bowl X?

60

11._____Which Raider returned an interception 75 yards for a touchdown and a record in Super Bowl XI?

12._____Which Cowboy running back threw a 29-yard touchdown pass to Golden Richards in Super Bowl XII?

13._____Who was the first quarterback to throw four touchdown passes in a Super Bowl game, in Super Bowl XIII?

14._____Who subbed for injured Ram quarterback Pat Haden in Super Bowl XIV?

15._____Who caught an 80-yard touchdown pass, the longest reception in Super Bowl history, in Super Bowl XV?

16._____Which Bengal set the Super Bowl reception record, with 11 catches for 104 yards, in Cincinnati's loss to the 49ers in Super Bowl XVI?

17._____Which Dolphin set the Super Bowl record with a 98-yard kickoff return for a touchdown in Super Bowl XVII?

18._____Which Raider linebacker intercepted Joe Theismann's pass and returned it five yards for a touchdown just before halftime in Super Bowl XVIII?

19._____Which 49er running back scored three touchdowns against Miami in Super Bowl XIX?

20._____Which Bear defensive tackle rushed for a touchdown in Super Bowl XX?

21._____Name the Giant tight end who caught four passes for 51 yards and a touchdown in Super Bowl XXI.

22._____Name the Redskin rookie who rushed for a Super Bowl–record 204 yards in Washington's victory over Denver in Super Bowl XXII.

23._____Which Bengal returned a kickoff 93

yards for a touchdown against San Francisco in Super Bowl XXIII?

24._____Name the 49er wide receiver who caught seven passes for 148 yards and three touchdowns in San Francisco's 55–10 demolition of Denver in Super Bowl XXIV.

25._____Name the Bill kicker who missed a potential game-winning 47-yard field goal against the Giants in Super Bowl XXV.

26._____Who threw a record 58 passes for Buffalo in Super Bowl XXVI?

27._____Which hot-dogging Cowboy, returning a fumble, was caught from behind and stripped of the ball by Buffalo's Don Beebe in Super Bowl XXVII?

28._____Name the Cowboy safety who forced a fumble, intercepted a pass, and returned a fumble for a touchdown in Dallas' win in Super Bowl XXVIII.

29._____Which Charger set a record with 242 yards on kickoff returns in Super Bowl XXIX?

30._____Which Cowboy defensive end recorded a sack in Super Bowl XXX, giving him a record 4½ sacks in Super Bowls?

II. GOING FOR THE RING

Match up each player in the left-hand column with the number of Super Bowl rings he has won, in the right-hand column. One player has won five; three, four; three, three; three, two; and five, one. The players with the same amount of rings are not in any special order.

1. Troy Aikman   (5) _____

2. Lawrence Taylor   (4) _____

3. Ronnie Lott   (4) _____

4. Joe Namath   (4) _____

5. Joe Theismann	(3)	_____
6. Charles Haley	(3)	_____
7. Joe Montana	(3)	_____
8. Bart Starr	(2)	_____
9. Ken Norton Jr.	(2)	_____
10. Terry Bradshaw	(2)	_____
11. Johnny Unitas	(1)	_____
12. Emmitt Smith	(1)	_____
13. Ken Stabler	(1)	_____
14. Walter Payton	(1)	_____
15. Jim Plunkett	(1)	_____

III. ONE-TIME WINNERS

Eight teams have won 26 of the 30 Super Bowls. The Cowboys and 49ers have each won five. The Steelers have copped four; the Redskins and Raiders, three; and the Packers, Giants, and Dolphins, two. Can you name the four one-time Super Bowl winners?

1. _____
2. _____
3. _____
4. _____

IV. SUPER BOWL MVPS

Can you figure out who were the following Super Bowl MVPs?

1. _____ I played quarterback for the University of Alabama and the Green Bay Packers. During my days in Green Bay, the team won six division crowns and five league titles, including victories in Super Bowls I and II. A Hall of Famer, I was named the MVP of those two Super Bowls. Who am I?

2._____I also played quarterback for Alabama. In the pros, I played with the Jets and the Rams, and was inducted into the Pro Football Hall of Fame in 1985. Did I mention that I was the MVP of Super Bowl III?

3._____A quarterback for Purdue University, I played with four pro teams, but made my mark with the Chiefs. In 1987, I was inducted into the Hall of Fame. My 28,711 career passing yards and 239 touchdown passes clinched my spot. By the way, I was the MVP of Super Bowl IV. Who am I?

4._____A center at the University of West Virginia, I was moved to outside linebacker during my 13 years with the Cowboys. To this day, I remain the only member of a losing team to win the MVP Award of a Super Bowl, winning it in the infamous "Blooper Bowl," otherwise known as Super Bowl V. Who am I?

5._____A former Heisman Trophy Award winner, I led the Cowboys to wins in Super Bowls VI and XII, winning the MVP Award in the former game. When I retired following the 1979 season, I had an 83.4 passing rating, the best rating ever at that time. Who am I?

6._____A defensive back with the Dolphins and Redskins, I played on the only undefeated team in NFL history. In Super Bowl VII, I had two interceptions, and was named the game's MVP. Who am I?

7._____The top draft pick of the Dolphins, I spent most of my years in Miami, but also a few with the Giants. In almost 2,000 career carries, I fumbled only 21 times. Oh, yes, I was the MVP of Super Bowl VIII. Who am I?

8._____A Penn State graduate, I played in four Super Bowls with the Steelers. MVP of Super Bowl IX, I finished my career with the Seahawks. I rushed for 1,556 yards in 19 postseason games. Who am I?

9._____An alumnus of USC, I played nine years in the NFL, and was known for my acrobatic catches.

My 64-yard touchdown reception in Super Bowl X secured the victory for the Steelers and the MVP Award for myself. Who am I?

10._____A Hall-of-Fame wide receiver, I corralled at least 40 catches in 10 straight seasons. Overall, I made 589 catches for 8,974 yards during my career. In Super Bowl XI, I caught four passes for 79 yards against the Vikings, and won the MVP Award in the Raiders' 32–14 victory. Who am I?

11._____I played my collegiate football at East Texas State, and went on to play defensive end for the Cowboys for 11 years.

The top draft choice for the Cowboys out of the University of Maryland, I played for Dallas for 14 years. In 1994 I was inducted into the Hall of Fame.

We were the co-MVPs of the Cowboys' Super Bowl XII triumph over the Broncos. Who are we?

12._____A quarterback for Louisiana Tech, I later played for four Super Bowl champions. Inducted into the Hall of Fame in 1989, I was the MVP of Super Bowls XIII and XIV. Who am I?

13._____A quarterback at Stanford University in college, and for the Patriots, the 49ers, and the Raiders in the NFL, I didn't become my team's starting signal caller until the sixth game in 1980, but I went on to become the MVP of Super Bowl XV. Who am I?

14._____I played college football at the University of Notre Dame and pro football from 1979 to 1994 with both the 49ers and the Chiefs. Known for leading my teams to many dramatic fourth-quarter victories, I was the MVP of Super Bowls XVI, XIX, and XXIV. Who am I?

15._____I began my pro football career with the Jets, but today I am remembered more for my play with the Redskins. Overall, I scored 104 touchdowns in my Hall-of-Fame career. I was the MVP of Super Bowl XVII. Who am I?

16._____A Heisman Trophy Award winner at the University of Southern California, I just completed my 14th year in the NFL. One of the most prolific scorers in NFL history, I won the MVP Award for my play with the Raiders in Super Bowl XVIII. Who am I?

17._____I played my collegiate ball at Tennessee State. Third on the NFL's all-time sack list with 126½, I was the MVP of Super Bowl XX with the Bears. Who am I?

18._____A graduate of Morehead State, I led my team to two Super Bowls, but played in just one of them, because of an injury. In Super Bowl XXI, though, I was named the game's MVP. I am now an NFL television commentator. Who am I?

19._____Groomed by coach Eddie Robinson at Grambling University, I became the first black quarterback to play in the Super Bowl. But I did more than play. Leading the Redskins to victory in Super Bowl XXII, I was named the MVP. Who am I?

20._____Drafted out of Mississippi Valley State in 1985, I currently have 10 consecutive seasons of 1,000-plus receiving yards, a league record. In Super Bowl XXIII, with the 49ers, I caught 11 passes for a Super Bowl record 215 yards, and I was named the game's MVP. Who am I?

21._____Out of the University of Miami, I played 14 years in the NFL and racked up 10,273 rushing yards, ninth on the all-time list. In Super Bowl XXV, with the Giants, I rushed for 102 yards and one touchdown to capture the MVP Award. Who am I?

22._____Currently playing for the St. Louis Rams, I was named the MVP of Super Bowl XXVI, when I completed 18 of 33 passes for the victorious Redskins. I became the third different quarterback to lead the Redskins to a Super Bowl victory under coach Joe Gibbs. Who am I?

23._____In 1995 I was named to my fifth consecutive Pro Bowl. A quarterback during the 1992 playoffs, I threw eight touchdown passes without an interception. In the 1994 NFC championship game, I passed for 380 yards. But my crowning moment was in Super Bowl XXVII, when I threw for 273 yards and four touchdowns, and was named the game's MVP. Who am I?

24._____A product of the University of Florida, I am the only player in NFL history to rush for 1,400 or more yards in five consecutive seasons. I was the MVP during the regular season in 1993, and the winner of the MVP in Super Bowl XXVIII. Who am I?

25._____I played for Brigham Young in college, the Los Angeles Express in the United States Football League, and the Buccaneers and the 49ers in the NFL. In 1994, I set the league record with a 112.8 quarterback rating. And, oh, how could I forget: I was the MVP of Super Bowl XXIX. Who am I?

26._____I played college football at Texas Christian University and was a twelfth-round draft choice of the Cowboys in 1991. In Super Bowl XXX I intercepted two passes for a Super Bowl record 76 yards and was named the game's MVP. Who am I?

CHAPTER THIRTEEN

THE ALL-AMERICAN FOOTBALL CONFERENCE AND THE AMERICAN FOOTBALL LEAGUE

THE ALL-AMERICAN FOOTBALL CONFERENCE

The All-American Football Conference (AAFC) was organized in 1946 by Arch Ward, the sports editor of the *Chicago Tribune*. In 1933, Ward had organized baseball's All-Star Game. Jim Crowley, one of the legendary backs from the "Four Horsemen" of Notre Dame, was the league's first commissioner.

The original eight teams were the New York Yankees, the Brooklyn Dodgers, the Buffalo Bisons, and the Miami Seahawks in the Eastern Division; and the Cleveland Browns, the Chicago Rockets, the San Francisco 49ers, and the Los Angeles Dons in the Western Division.

After four years of intense high-profile bidding, the NFL and the AAFC merged, at the end of the 1949 season. The Browns, the Colts, the Yankees, and the 49ers were admitted from the AAFC into the NFL. The other AAFC teams were disbanded, and their players were put into a pool and distributed among the NFL teams.

The Colts' franchise folded after a disastrous 1950 NFL season. After the 1951 campaign, the Yankees moved to Dallas, becoming the Texans; and after the 1952 season, the Texans moved back to Baltimore, becoming the Colts.

I. THE AAFC

Select the correct answer from the four multiple-choice possibilities in this All-American Football Conference quiz.

1._____In the 1946 title game, the Browns de-

feated the Yankees, 14–9. Identify the Brown who rushed 13 times for 98 yards and a touchdown.
A. Marion Motley, B. Bill Willis, C. Dub Jones, or D. Ernest Byner.

2._____In 1947, Cleveland again defeated New York, 14–3. Name the quarterback who rushed for the game's first touchdown.
A. Frank Ryan, B. Otto Graham, C. Brian Sipe, or D. Vinny Testaverde

3._____Who won the 1948 title by a 49–7 score over Buffalo?
A. Cleveland Browns, B. New York Yankees, C. San Francisco 49ers, or D. Chicago Rockets

4._____In the final AAFC title game, in 1949, the Browns won, 21–7. Whom did they beat?
A. New York Yankees, B. Los Angeles Dons, C. Chicago Rockets, or D. San Francisco 49ers

5._____In 1948, the 49ers gained a pro football record 3,663 yards rushing. Name the future Hall of Famer who contributed to this effort in his rookie year.
A. Roger Craig, B. Johnny Strzkolski, C. Joe Perry, or D. Hugh McElhenny

6._____Which Hall-of-Fame halfback, receiver, and defensive back played for the Rockets from 1946 to 1948?
A. Frank Gifford, B. Elroy "Crazy Legs" Hirsch, C. Spec Sanders, or D. Earl Campbell

7._____The "Bald Eagle," he played with the Colts in 1948 and 1949.
A. Y. A. Tittle, B. Sammy Baugh, C. Cliff Harris, or D. Dub Jones

8._____This defensive tackle played for the 1948–49 Yankees and later went on to be a four-time All-NFL selection, and a Hall of Famer.
A. Bill Willis, B. Art Donovan, C. Arnie Weinmeister, or D. Tony Tolbert

9._____In 1948, this baseball owner purchased the Brooklyn Dodgers of the AAFC. His patience with the franchise lasted only for one year, however. Who was that owner who sold the club back to the league after only one year?
A. George Steinbrenner, B. Walter O'Malley, C. Branch Rickey, or D. Dan Topping

10._____This quarterback was the NFL's MVP in 1940 as a member of the Brooklyn Dodgers. In 1946, he was the Yankees' signal caller in the AAFC. Who is he?
A. Y. A. Tittle, B. Otto Graham, C. Cecil Isbell, or D. Clarence "Ace" Parker

THE AMERICAN FOOTBALL LEAGUE

The American Football League, whose chief organizer was Lamar Hunt of Dallas, began play in 1960 with eight teams. The teams were located in Boston, Buffalo, Dallas, Denver, Houston, Los Angeles, New York City, and Oakland.

The teams added three innovations to appeal to the fans. First, they adopted a two-point conversion alternative for the extra point(s). Second, they placed the players' names on the backs of their football jerseys. And third, they made the scoreboard clock the official time.

Joe Foss, a former pilot and governor of South Dakota, was appointed as the first commissioner.

A draft similar to the NFL's was instituted. The AFL scored its first victory when the courts declared Billy Cannon's contract with the Rams invalid. He had been the NFL's first draft pick in 1960. Cannon, a Heisman Trophy Award winner at Louisiana State University, then signed with Houston in the AFL.

On June 8, 1966, Commissioner Pete Rozelle of the NFL announced a merger between the two leagues. The two leagues agreed to a championship game between themselves, starting with the 1966 season.

II. Did They Play in the AFL?

Ten of the 20 players listed below spent at least part of their careers in the AFL. Which ones?

George Blanda
Dick Butkus
Jim Brown
Jerry Mays
Lance Alworth
Ken Stabler
Bob Griese
Bob Lilly
Paul Hornung
Cookie Gilchrist

Terry Bradshaw
Charlie Joiner
O. J. Simpson
Fran Tarkenton
Bill Bergey
Ahmad Rashad
Larry Csonka
Ollie Matson
Charley Taylor
Ken Houston

1._____
2._____
3._____
4._____
5._____

6._____
7._____
8._____
9._____
10._____

III. AFL Truths or Falsehoods

Answer the following questions as either True or False.

1._____The New York Jets were originally called the New York Titans.

2._____Pete Rozelle was the first commissioner of the AFL.

3._____The Miami Dolphins were one of the AFL's original eight teams.

4._____Al Davis was a commissioner of the AFL.

5._____Sid Gillman was the head coach and the general manager of the San Diego Chargers.

6._____Nick Buoniconti played for the Boston Patriots.

7._____The Oakland Raiders were the second AFL team to win a Super Bowl.

8._____The AFL started the practice of putting players' names on the backs of their jerseys.

9._____Joe Namath led the New York Jets to three AFL titles.

10._____Cookie Gilchrist played for the San Diego Chargers.

IV. PICK THE WINNER

The respective teams in the AFL championship games from 1960 to 1969 are paired below. All you have to do is pick the winner.

1. Houston Oilers vs. Los Angeles Chargers (1960)

_____

2. Houston Oilers vs. San Diego Chargers (1961)

_____

3. Dallas Texans vs. Houston Oilers (1962)

_____

4. San Diego Chargers vs. Boston Patriots (1963)

_____

5. Buffalo Bills vs. San Diego Chargers (1964)

_____

6. Buffalo Bills vs. San Diego Chargers (1965)

_____

7. Kansas City Chiefs vs. Buffalo Bills (1966)

_____

8. Oakland Raiders vs. Houston Oilers (1967)

_____

9. Oakland Raiders vs. New York Jets (1968)

_____

10. Oakland Raiders vs. Kansas City Chiefs (1969)

_____

CHAPTER FOURTEEN

THE HALL OF FAME

I. HALL OF FAMERS

Match the 20 Hall of Famers listed below with their descriptions that follow.

Jim Brown	Gino Marchetti
Larry Wilson	Lenny Moore
Wayne Millner	Sammy Baugh
Alan Page	Mike Ditka
Joe Namath	Paul Warfield
Randy White	Mel Blount
George Connor	Norm Van Brocklin
Sam Huff	Charley Taylor
Ray Nitschke	Sid Luckman
Jack Lambert	Johnny Unitas

1. _____This Boston and Washington Redskin receiver had 55- and 78-yard touchdown receptions in the 1937 championship game.

2. _____He was a Colt who scored touchdowns in a record 18 consecutive games between 1963 and 1965.

3. _____A former Bear, Eagle, and Cowboy, in 1988 he became the first tight end to be inducted into the Pro Football Hall of Fame.

4. _____A Brown, he led the league in rushing in eight of his nine seasons in the league.

5. _____This hard-hitting cornerback played on four Super Bowl champs. He was the MVP on defense in 1975.

6. _____He was a Hall-of-Fame charter enshrinee, and a six-time NFL passing leader. He was also the league's passing, punting, and interception leader in 1943.

7. _____In 1967, he became the first quarterback to pass for more than 4,000 yards in one season. In Super Bowl III he led the Jets over the Colts.

8. _____An NFL iron man, he played in 236 consecutive games, four Super Bowls, and was the league

MVP in 1971. A defensive tackle, he played for the Vikings and the Bears.

9. _____This Brown and Dolphin was the key to every offense he played on. He racked up 8,565 career receiving yards, scored 85 touchdowns, and earned a Pro Bowl spot eight times.

10. _____This Cowboy played 14 seasons, was a Pro Bowler nine times, and was named co-MVP of Super Bowl XII. (Harvey Martin, a teammate, shared MVP honors with him that day.)

11. _____This Redskin was the Rookie of the Year as a running back. Later, he was switched to wide receiver and ended up winning reception titles in both 1966 and 1967.

12. _____He passed for a record 554 yards in the 1951 league opener. In 1960, he led the Eagles to the league title while winning MVP honors.

13. _____This cunning Cardinal had 52 career interceptions, including one in each of seven consecutive games in 1966. Also, he made the "safety blitz" popular.

14. _____One of the most feared players of his era, this Steeler middle linebacker was the force behind the "Steel Curtain." A two-time Defensive Player of the Year, he played in nine Pro Bowl games.

15. _____A Dallas Texan and Baltimore Colt, he was named the top defensive end of the NFL's first 50 years. He played in 11 consecutive Pro Bowl games and made all-league honors seven times.

16. _____This Packer was the MVP of the 1962 title game. He was named the league's all-time linebacker in 1969. Known as an intimidator on the field, he was very low-key off it.

17. _____He passed for 40,239 yards and 290 touchdowns. He also led the Colts to two league championships and threw at least one touchdown in a record 47 consecutive games.

18. _____In the history of the NFL, only one man has been named All-Pro on both offense and defense in

the same year. This Bear tackle and linebacker accomplished the feat three years in a row, from 1951 to 1953.

19. _____In 1943, this Bear quarterback threw seven touchdown passes in one game and was named the league's MVP. A graduate of Columbia University, he made all-league five times.

20. _____This "Man in the Middle" played for the Giants and Redskins. He intercepted 30 passes and played in six NFL title games and five Pro Bowl contests.

II. CAN YOU PICK OUT THE HALL OF FAMERS?

Fifty standout professional football players are listed below. Only 25 of them are in the Hall of Fame, however. Do you know which ones? The answers do not have to be placed in any specific order.

Charley Taylor	Fred Dryer
D. D. Lewis	Chuck Foreman
Fred Biletnikoff	L. C. Greenwood
Bob Griese	Emlen Tunnell
Irv Cross	Paul Krause
Tobin Rote	O. J. Simpson
John Stallworth	Jim Langer
Dave Casper	Don Maynard
Larry Csonka	Lee Roy Jordan
Herb Adderley	Bill Bergey
Frank Gifford	Alan Page
Otto Graham	Mel Renfro
Drew Pearson	Ken Anderson
Jim Plunkett	Roman Gabriel
Bert Jones	Jim Marshall
Art Shell	Steve Largent
Ken Stabler	Raymond Berry
Len Dawson	Emmitt Thomas
Lee Roy Selmon	Doak Walker
Chuck Bednarik	Gary Collins

Jim Parker   Mike Curtis
Lyle Alzado   Willie Wood
Joe Greene   Ed "Too Tall" Jones
Charlie Joiner   Jan Stenerud
Jack Tatum   Jackie Smith

1. _____
2. _____
3. _____
4. _____
5. _____
6. _____
7. _____
8. _____
9. _____
10. _____
11. _____
12. _____
13. _____
14. _____
15. _____
16. _____
17. _____
18. _____
19. _____
20. _____
21. _____
22. _____
23. _____
24. _____
25. _____

PIGSKIN POTPOURRI

I. DRAFT CHOICES

Name the teams that originally drafted these stars who went on to successful careers with other organizations.

1. Brett Favre   _____
2. Bo Jackson   _____
3. John Elway   _____
4. Jeff George   _____
5. Vinny Testaverde   _____
6. Jim Plunkett   _____
7. Dick ("Night Train") Lane   _____
8. Bobby Mitchell   _____
9. Ted Hendricks   _____
10. Doug Atkins   _____
11. Deion Sanders   _____
12. Chuck Howley   _____
13. Jim Everett   _____
14. Cornelius Bennett   _____
15. Sean Jones   _____
16. Chuck Muncie   _____
17. Wes Chandler   _____
18. George Connor   _____
19. John Riggins   _____
20. Len Dawson   _____
21. Jay Novacek   _____
22. Fred Dryer   _____
23. Stan Humphries   _____
24. Andre Rison   _____
25. John Matuszak   _____

II. PLAYERS AND THEIR BIRTHPLACES

Match the players in the left-hand column with their places of birth in the right-hand column.

1. _ Dan Fouts   A. Bronx, New York

2. _ Bob Griese   B. Starkville, Mississippi

3. _ Rodney Hampton C. New Eagle, Pennsylvania

4. _ Bruce Smith   D. Shreveport, Louisiana

5. _ Johnny Unitas   E. Pensacola, Florida

6. _ Jerry Rice   F. Norfolk, Virginia

7. _ Art Donovan   G. Santa Monica, California

8. _ Ronnie Lott   H. Los Angeles, California

9. _ Frank Gifford   I. Salt Lake City, Utah

10. _ Terry Bradshaw   J. San Francisco, California

11. _ Bronko Nagurski K. Houston, Texas

12. _ Joe Namath   L. Evansville, Indiana

13. _ Hugh McElhenny M. Rainy River, Ontario, Canada

14. _ Jan Stenerud   N. Pass Christian, Mississippi

15. _ Jim Thorpe   O. Pittsburgh, Pennsylvania

16. _ Barry Sanders   P. Albuquerque, New Mexico

17. _ Deion Sanders   Q. Wichita, Kansas

18. _ Randy White   R. Fetsund, Norway

19. _ Joe Montana   S. Fort Myers, Florida

20. _ Brett Favre   T. Wilmington, Delaware

21. _ Rod Woodson   U. Philadelphia, Pennsylvania

22. _ Doak Walker   V. Prague, Oklahoma

23. _ Steve Young   W. Dallas, Texas

24. _ Leroy Kelly   X. Beaver Falls, Pennsylvania

25. _ Emmitt Smith   Y. Fort Wayne, Indiana

III. MATCHING NAMES

Match the following players with their nicknames.

Ken Stabler	Jack Tatum
Roger Staubach	William Perry
Skip Thomas	Gerald McNeil

Deion Sanders
Elroy Hirsch
John Matuszak
Ted Hendricks
Thomas Henderson
John Fuqua
Willie Anderson
John Elliot
Craig Heyward
Steve McMichael
Eddie Payton
Walter Payton

Johnny Jones
Billy Johnson
Fred Williamson
Paul Hornung
Lance Alworth
Joe Greene
Gary Johnson
Sam Cunningham
Ray Hamilton
Raghib Ismail
Pat Fischer
Dennis Winston

1. "Flipper" _____

2. "Jumbo" _____

3. "White Shoes" _____

4. "Mongo" _____

5. "Sugar Bear" _____

6. "Hollywood" _____

7. "Ice Cube" _____

8. "The Refrigerator" _____

9. "Sweetness" _____

10. "Assasin" _____

11. "Lam" _____

12. "Rocket" _____

13. "Bambi" _____

14. "The Hammer" _____

15. "Bam" _____

16. "Frenchy" _____

17. "Mad Stork" _____

18. "Iron Head" _____

19. "Big Hands" _____

20. "Mean Joe" _____

21. "The Golden Boy" _____

22. "Sweet P" _____

23. "Tooz" _____

24. "Crazy Legs" _____

25. "Dr. Death" _____

26. "Dirt" _____

27. "Mouse" _____

28. "Snake" _____

29. "Neon Deion" _____

30. "The Dodger" _____

IV. TEAM NICKNAMES

Match the team in the left-hand column with its nickname in the right-hand column.

1. _____ Dolphins   A. "Cardiac Kids"

2. _____ Broncos   B. "Umbrella Defense"

3. _____ Cowboys   C. "No-Name Defense"

4. _____ Steelers   D. "Orange Crush"

5. _____ Vikings   E. "Steel Curtain"

6. _____ Bears   F. "Over-the-Hill Gang"

7. _____ Rams   G. "Doomsday Defense"

8. _____ Giants   H. "Fearsome Foursome"

9. _____ Browns   I. "Monsters of the Midway"

10. _____ Redskins   J. "Purple People Eaters"

V. STADIUMS

Match the teams in the left-hand column with the stadiums they used to play in, listed in the right-hand column.

1. San Francisco 49ers   __ A. Yankee Stadium

2. Buffalo Bills   __ B. Shea Stadium

3. Minnesota Vikings	_ C.	Cotton Bowl
4. Baltimore Colts	_ D.	War Memorial Stadium
5. Houston Oilers	_ E.	Shibe Park
6. Atlanta Falcons	_ F.	Kezar Stadium
7. Chicago Cardinals	_ G.	Schaefer Stadium
8. Dallas Cowboys	_ H.	Metropolitan Stadium
9. New York Jets	_ I.	Memorial Stadium
10. New York Giants	_ J.	Rice Stadium
11. Detroit Lions	_ K.	Orange Bowl
12. New England Patriots	_ L.	Busch Memorial Stadium
13. Philadelphia Eagles	_ M.	Fulton County Stadium
14. St. Louis Cardinals	_ N.	Comiskey Park
15. Miami Dolphins	_ O.	Briggs Stadium

VI. PAST AND PRESENT TRUTHS OR FALSEHOODS

Respond to the following statements with a true or false answer.

1._____Bob Waterfield was the MVP as a rookie in 1945, and he led the (Cleveland) Rams to the league title that year.

2._____Emlen Tunnell gained more yards on kickoff returns and interceptions (923) in 1952 than that season's rushing leader.

3._____Tom Landry played defensive back for the Giants.

4._____Johnny Lujack was inducted into the Pro Football Hall of Fame.

5._____Johnny Lujack beat out Doak Walker for the 1950 league-scoring title, 128–109.

6._____In 1953 the Dallas Texans, who had joined the NFL the previous year, moved to Baltimore and adopted the Colts as their nickname.

7._____Hall-of-Famer Chuck Bednarik played linebacker as well as center on both sides of the ball.

8._____Doak Walker played his college ball at the University of Texas.

9._____Lou Groza kicked a 16-yard field goal to defeat the Los Angeles Rams, 30–28, to give the Browns the 1950 championship.

10._____Charlie Trippi was a Hall-of-Fame halfback for the Giants.

11._____Larry Wilson of the Cardinals made the "safety blitz" famous.

12._____Hall of Famer Willie Wood competed in three Super Bowls.

13._____Vince Lombardi's teams never lost a league championship game.

14._____Jack Butler tied a league record when he set the Steelers' single-game interception mark with four thefts.

15._____Dick Shiner led the Steelers in passing in both 1968 and 1969.

16._____Frank Gifford's number "16" has been retired by the Giants.

17._____Del Shofner holds the Giants' single-game receiving record with 269 yards.

18._____Johnny Unitas started Super Bowl III at quarterback for the Colts.

19._____Johnny Unitas played in back-to-back Super Bowls.

20._____Paul Hornung played in Super Bowl I for the Packers.

21._____In the first AFL championship game (1961), the Oilers defeated the Chargers, 24–16.

22._____In Super Bowl III, Tom Matte of the

Colts and Matt Snell of the Jets each rushed for over 100 yards.

23._____Jim Brown beat out Jimmy Taylor for the 1962 rushing title.

24._____The Cowboys beat the Dolphins in the second week of the 1973 season to halt Miami's regular-season winning streak at 16.

25._____The NFL goal posts were moved from the goal line to the back of the end zone at the beginning of the 1974 season.

26._____Tom Morrow of the Raiders inter-cepted a pass in a league-record eight consecutive games.

27._____Super Bowl IX, between the Vikings and the Steelers, was played at the Superdome.

28._____Earl "Curley" Lambeau is the Cardi-nals' all-time winning coach.

29._____Joe Montana holds the record for the most seasons leading the league in passing.

30._____Walter Payton won the most rushing titles with eight.

31._____Tony Dorsett never played on a Super Bowl winner.

32._____Eric Dickerson and Walter Payton are the only two backs to rush for 2,000 yards in a season.

33._____Buddy Ryan as a head coach never won a playoff game.

34._____Joe Gibbs coached more Super Bowl winning teams than Tom Landry.

35._____The Jets have appeared in two Super Bowls.

36._____Everson Walls is the only player to lead the league in interceptions three times.

37._____Joe Montana has the highest career pass rating.

38._____Drew Bledsoe threw 70 passes in one game, a league record.

39._____Ken Anderson's 70.55 completion percentage in 1982 is the league's all-time best.

40._____The Raiders have won two Super Bowl titles.

41._____Tom Flores is the Raiders' all-time winning coach.

42._____Ken Stabler threw more than 200 touchdown passes in his career.

43._____The 49ers have never lost a Super Bowl game.

44._____Paul Krause holds the league lead with 81 career interceptions.

45._____No head coach has won four Super Bowl games.

46._____Steve Young owns the San Francisco single-season record with 35 touchdown passes.

47._____No coach in Tampa Bay history has a winning record.

48._____Rich Karlis shares the league record with seven field goals in one game.

49._____Mike Garrett is the Chiefs' all-time leading rusher.

50._____Len Dawson holds the Chiefs' single-season passing yardage record with 4,348 yards.

VII. Retired Numbers

Match the players in the left-hand column with their retired numbers in the right-hand column.

1. Otto Graham	_____	A. 12
2. Johnny Unitas	_____	B. 3
3. Art Donovan	_____	C. 74
4. Bob Griese	_____	D. 14
5. Larry Wilson	_____	E. 34
6. Don Maynard	_____	F. 37
7. Bronko Nagurski	_____	G. 19
8. Walter Payton	_____	H. 13
9. Doak Walker	_____	I. 8
10. Ray Nitschke	_____	J. 70
11. Lawrence Taylor	_____	K. 60
12. Fran Tarkenton	_____	L. 99
13. Chuck Bednarik	_____	M. 56
14. Merlin Olsen	_____	N. 7
15. Hugh McElhenny	_____	O. 66
16. Steve Van Buren	_____	P. 40
17. Gayle Sayers	_____	Q. 51
18. Dick Butkus	_____	R. 39
19. Jerome Brown	_____	S. 10
20. Bob Waterfield	_____	T. 15

VIII. PRO FOOTBALL DID YOU KNOW....

....Paul Krause, a defensive back for the Redskins and the Vikings, had 81 career interceptions, the league's all-time high in that category? But he is *not* in the Hall of Fame.

*****

....the 1940 championship game between the Bears and the Redskins was the first title contest to be carried on network radio? Chicago defeated Washington in the most lopsided contest in NFL history, 73–0. Red Barber broadcast the game.

*****

.... Tony Canadeo of the Packers and Steve Van Buren of the Eagles each rushed for more than 1,000 yards in 1949? It was the first time the NFL produced two 1,000-yard rushers in the same season.

*****

.... George Allen, head coach of the Los Angeles Rams and the Redskins, coined the term "Nickel Defense"? Outside of 1972, when he led the Redskins to the Super Bowl, his teams were 0–6 in the playoffs.

*****

.... ABC began televising "Monday Night Football" with a 13-game package in 1970?

*****

.... the winner's share for the 1933 NFL champion Bears was $210.34 a player?

*****

.... Jimmy Johnson and Barry Switzer have been the only two coaches to win a national collegiate championship and a Super Bowl title?

*****

.... nine receivers caught 100 or more passes in 1995, and all of them were from the NFC?

*****

.... George Halas was the Yankee right fielder the year before Babe Ruth arrived in New York?

*****

.... Paul Brown invented the face mask?

*****

.... quarterback Gail Gilbert was on the roster of five consec-

86

utive losing teams in the Super Bowl, the 1990–93 Bills and the 1994 Chargers?

*****

.... the Redskins lost the 1945 title game because of a strong wind, the goal post, and an odd rule? Early in the first quarter, Washington quarterback Sammy Baugh dropped back to pass in his own end zone, but when he let the ball go, a gust of wind blew it into the goal post, and the ball bounced back into the end zone, which was a two-point safety under the rules then in effect. The Cleveland Rams went on to defeat the Redskins, 15–14.

*****

.... the Cowboys had a string of 20 consecutive winning seasons from 1966 to 1985? Only the New York Yankees, who had a 39-year streak from 1926 to 1964, and the Montreal Canadiens, who had a 32-year skein from 1952 to 1983, put together longer strings of consecutive winning seasons in professional sports history.

*****

.... in 1992, there were a record nine new head coaches in the NFL? Five of them were first-time head coaches. Three of those five, Pittsburgh's Bill Cowher, Minnesota's Dennis Green, and San Diego's Bobby Ross, led their clubs to division titles.

*****

.... Chicago Cardinal quarterback Jim Hardy had a record eight passes intercepted in a game against the 1950 Philadelphia Eagles?

*****

.... Johnny Unitas and Dan Marino have the same middle name—Constantine?

*****

.... Ken Norton Jr. has been the only player to perform on

three consecutive Super Bowl winners? He played with the 1992–93 Cowboys and the 1994 49ers.

*****

.... the Giants tied the Eagles in the last pro football game played at Yankee Stadium, 23–23?

*****

.... Bernie Kosar of the Browns holds the NFL record for most consecutive passes thrown (308) without an interception?

*****

.... former Viking kicker Fred Cox booted at least one field goal in a league-record 31 consecutive games?

*****

.... John Elway in 1994 became the first quarterback in league history to have a pass intercepted and returned for a touchdown in each of the first three games of the season: against the Chargers, Jets, and Raiders, all losses?

*****

.... Bret Perriman of the Lions became the first player in NFL history to score a pair of two-point conversions in the same game when he did it against Green Bay in 1994, the first year that the two-point "extra point" was in effect in the "old league"?

*****

.... the Dallas Cowboys hold the NFL all-time record for postseason wins with 31? The Redskins, Raiders, and 49ers are tied for second with 21.

*****

.... none of the 30 Super Bowl games has gone into overtime?

*****

....Fullback William Floyd of the 49ers scored five touch-downs in the 1994 postseason, the most by any rookie in NFL history?

*****

....NFL Charities donated $1 million through United Way to victims of the Bay Area earthquake in 1989? A non-profit organization, NFL Charities was created in 1973.

*****

....Adrian Burk of the Eagles threw seven touchdowns in one game in 1994 to tie Sid Luckman's record? In 1969, Burk was working a game as an NFL official when Joe Kapp of the Vikings also fired seven touchdowns. George Blanda and Y. A. Tittle have also thrown for seven six-pointers in one game.

Chapter One Answers

I. Present-Day Players

A. Troy Aikman, of the Dallas Cowboys

B. Drew Bledsoe, of the New England Patriots

C. Larry Centers, of the Arizona Cardinals

D. Richard Dent, of the Chicago Bears. (He tied with Rich Milot of the 1984 Redskins.)

E. John Elway, of the Denver Broncos

F. Marshall Faulk, of the Indianapolis Colts

G. James Geathers, of the Atlanta Falcons

H. Ken Harvey, of the Washington Redskins

I. Michael Irvin, of the Dallas Cowboys

J. Daryl Johnston, of the Dallas Cowboys

K. Jim Kelly, of the Buffalo Bills

L. Ronnie Lott, of the San Francisco 49ers

M. Willie McGinest, of the New England Patriots

N. Jay Novacek, of the Dallas Cowboys

O. Louis Oliver, of the Miami Dolphins. (Vencie Glenn of the 1987 Chargers did it first.)

P. Bryce Paup, of the Buffalo Bills

Q. Jeff Query, of the Cincinnati Bengals

R. Andre Reed. (Ten other players have performed the feat.)

S. Deion Sanders. (The 1992 World Series with the Atlanta Braves, and the 1994 and '95 Super Bowls with the San Francisco 49ers and Dallas Cowboys, respectively.)

T. John Taylor

U. Jeff Uhlenhake

V. Tommy Vardell

W. Ricky Watters, of the San Francisco 49ers

Y. Steve Young, of the San Francisco 49ers, in 1994

Z. Tony Zendejas, of the Los Angeles Rams

II. Yesterday's Heroes

A. Dick Anderson
B. Raymond Berry
C. Jack Christiansen. (Rick Upchurch of the Broncos has since tied the mark.)
D. Al Davis
E. Herman Edwards
F. Dan Fortmann
G. Red Grange
H. George Halas
I. Cecil Isbell
J. Deacon Jones
K. Leroy Kelly
L. Bobby Layne
M. John Mackey
N. Earle "Greasy" Neale
O. Jim Otto
P. Don Perkins
R. Art Rooney
S. O. J. Simpson
T. Fran Tarkenton
U. Gene Upshaw
V. Steve Van Buren
W. Charlie Waters. (Bill Simpson of the Rams and Bills and Ronnie Lott of the 49ers, Raiders, and Jets also have nine.)
Y. Ron Yary
Z. Jim Zorn

III. Famous Postseason Games and Players

1. D	4. H	7. I	10. E
2. F	5. G	8. J	
3. A	6. B	9. C	

Chapter Two Answers

I. Quarterbacks with 4,000-Yard Passing Seasons

1. Dan Marino (6 seasons)
2. Warren Moon (4 seasons)
3. Dan Fouts (3 seasons)
4. Joe Namath (1 season)
5. Phil Simms (1 season)

II. Quarterbacks with 400-Yard Passing Games

1. Dan Marino (13 games)
2. Dan Fouts (6 games)
3. Dave Krieg (4 games)
4. Tommy Kramer (4 games)
5. Joe Namath (3 games)

III. All-Time Club-Leading NFC Quarterbacks

1. Jim Hart
2. Steve Bartkowski
3. Kerry Collins
4. Sid Luckman
5. Roger Staubach
6. Bobby Layne
7. Bart Starr
8. Fran Tarkenton
9. Archie Manning
10. Phil Simms
11. Ron Jaworski
12. Jim Everett
13. Joe Montana
14. Vinny Testaverde
15. Joe Theismann

IV. All-Time Club-Leading AFC Quarterbacks

1. Jim Kelly
2. Ken Anderson
3. Brian Sipe
4. John Elway
5. Warren Moon
6. Johnny Unitas
7. Mark Brunell
8. Len Dawson
9. Dan Marino
10. Steve Grogan
11. Joe Namath
12. Ken Stabler
13. Terry Bradshaw
14. Dan Fouts
15. Dave Krieg

V. Quarterbacks and Their Alma Maters

1. G
2. K
3. H
4. J
5. C
6. D
7. N
8. O
9. M
10. A
11. I
12. F
13. E
14. L
15. B

VI. Touchdown Tandems

1. J	6. A	11. S	16. F
2. Q	7. M	12. R	17. O
3. I	8. D	13. G	18. N
4. B	9. K	14. P	19. T
5. H	10. E	15. C	20. L

Chapter Three Answers

I. NFC Team All-Time Rushing Leaders

1. Ottis Anderson
2. Gerald Riggs
3. Derrick Moore
4. Walter Payton
5. Tony Dorsett
6. Barry Sanders
7. Jim Taylor
8. Chuck Foreman
9. George Rogers
10. Rodney Hampton
11. Wilbert Montgomery
12. Eric Dickerson
13. Joe Perry
14. James Wilder
15. John Riggins

II. AFC Team All-Time Rushing Leaders

1. O. J. Simpson
2. James Brooks
3. Jim Brown
4. Floyd Little
5. Earl Campbell
6. Lydell Mitchell
7. James Stewart
8. Christian Okoye
9. Larry Csonka
10. Sam Cunningham
11. Freeman McNeil
12. Marcus Allen
13. Franco Harris
14. Paul Lowe
15. Curt Warner

III. Rushing-Title Leaders

1. Jim Brown (8 titles)
2. O. J. Simpson (4 titles)
3. Eric Dickerson (4 titles)
4. Earl Campbell (3 titles)
5. George Rogers (1 title)

IV. Running Backs and Their Records

1. Tony Dorsett (1983 Dallas Cowboys)
2. Earl Campbell (1980 Houston Oilers)
3. Eric Dickerson (1984 Los Angeles Rams)
4. Jim Brown (Cleveland Browns)
5. John Riggins (1982–83 Washington Redskins)
6. Emmitt Smith (1995 Dallas Cowboys)
7. Walter Payton (Chicago Bears)
8. O. J. Simpson
9. Marcus Allen (1985–86 Oakland Raiders)
10. Gayle Sayers (1965 Chicago Bears)
11. Thurman Thomas (Buffalo Bills). He tied Kellen Winslow of the 1981 San Diego Chargers. Shannon Sharpe of the 1993 Broncos has also tied the mark.
12. Franco Harris (1972 Pittsburgh Steelers)
13. Jim Taylor (Green Bay Packers)
14. Barry Sanders (Detroit Lions)
15. Ottis Anderson (five times with the St. Louis Cardinals, and once with the New York Giants)

V. Running Backs and Their Alma Maters

1. D	6. J	11. M
2. F	7. B	12. O
3. G	8. E	13. I
4. A	9. H	14. N
5. C	10. L	15. K

Chapter Four Answers

I. NFC Team All-Time Receiving-Yardage Leaders

1. Roy Green
2. Andre Rison
3. Mark Carrier
4. Johnny Morris
5. Michael Irvin
6. Gail Cogdill
7. James Lofton
8. Anthony Carter
9. Eric Martin
10. Frank Gifford
11. Harold Carmichael
12. Henry Ellard
13. Jerry Rice
14. Mark Carrier
15. Art Monk

II. AFC Team All-Time Receiving-Yardage Leaders

1. Andre Reed
2. Isaac Curtis
3. Ozzie Newsome
4. Lionel Taylor
5. Ernest Givens
6. Raymond Berry
7. Willie Jackson
8. Otis Taylor
9. Mark Duper
10. Stanley Morgan
11. Don Maynard
12. Fred Biletnikoff
13. John Stallworth
14. Lance Alworth
15. Steve Largent

III. NFC Team All-Time Reception Leaders

1. Roy Green
2. Andre Rison
3. Mark Carrier
4. Walter Payton
5. Michael Irvin
6. Charlie Sanders
7. Sterling Sharpe
8. Steve Jordan
9. Eric Martin
10. Joe Morrison
11. Harold Carmichael
12. Henry Ellard
13. Jerry Rice
14. James Wilder
15. Art Monk

IV. AFC Team All-Time Reception Leaders

1. Andre Reed
2. Chris Collinsworth
3. Ozzie Newsome
4. Lionel Taylor
5. Ernest Givens
6. Raymond Berry
7. Willie Jackson
8. Henry Marshall
9. Mark Clayton
10. Stanley Morgan
11. Don Maynard
12. Fred Biletnikoff
13. John Stallworth
14. Charlie Joiner
15. Steve Largent

V. Receivers' Reunion

1. G	9. C
2. I	10. H
3. A	11. B
4. F	12. K
5. O	13. D
6. M	14. E
7. J	15. L
8. N	

VI. Royal Receivers

1. Jerry Rice (ten 1,000-yard seasons)
2. Steve Largent (eight 1,000-yard seasons)
3. Lance Alworth (seven 1,000-yard seasons)
4. Michael Irvin (five 1,000-yard seasons)
5. Art Powell (five 1,000-yard seasons)

VII. Touchdown Twins

1. Jerry Rice (146 touchdown receptions)
2. Steve Largent (100 touchdown receptions)
3. Don Maynard (88 touchdown receptions)
4. Tommy McDonald (84 touchdown receptions)
5. Art Powell (81 touchdown receptions)
6. Harold Carmichael (79 touchdown receptions)
7. Charley Taylor (79 touchdown receptions)
8. Harold Jackson (76 touchdown receptions)
9. Nat Moore (74 touchdown receptions)
10. Stanley Morgan (72 touchdown receptions)
11. Bob Hayes (71 touchdown receptions)
12. Wesley Walker (71 touchdown receptions)
13. Gary Collins (70 touchdown receptions)
14. Art Monk (68 touchdown receptions)
15. Sterling Sharpe (65 touchdown receptions)

Chapter Five Answers

I. Leading the Way

1. J	6. A	11. D
2. O	7. N	12. E
3. H	8. B	13. K
4. I	9. C	14. G
5. L	10. F	15. M

II. In the Trenches

1. True. (He played as a tackle in 1935, and as a guard in 1937.)
2. True
3. False. (Hannah played in Super Bowl XX.)
4. False. (He became a charter enshrinee in 1963.)
5. False. (He played tackle.)
6. False
7. True
8. False. (The Redskin offensive line of the 1980s was called "The Hogs.")
9. True. (He was enshrined in 1964.)
10. True. (He appeared in the Pro Bowls from 1989 to 95.)
11. True
12. False. (Lowdermilk played for the Vikings.)
13. False. (Webb played for Texas A&M.)
14. True
15. True

III. Famous "Front Fours"

1. Lamar Lundy	6. Alex Karras
2. L. C. Greenwood	7. Art Donovan
3. Gary Larsen	8. Jim Katcavage
4. Harvey Martin	9. Buck Buchanan
5. Dick Hudson	10. Steve McMichael

IV. Twenty Tough Tight Ends

1. John Mackey
2. Jay Novacek
3. Kellen Winslow
4. Todd Christensen
5. Shannon Sharpe
6. Brent Jones
7. Mike Ditka
8. Jackie Smith
9. Ozzie Newsome
10. Mark Bavaro
11. Russ Francis
12. Dave Casper
13. Leon Hart
14. Bob Tucker
15. Jerry Smith
16. Pete Retzlaff
17. Ben Coates
18. Riley Odoms
19. Jimmie Giles
20. Billy Joe Dupree

Chapter Six Answers

I. Who's Who

1. Sam Huff
2. Lawrence Taylor
3. Joe Schmidt
4. Willie Lanier
5. Jack Lambert
6. Ted Hendricks
7. Bill George
8. Mike Singletary
9. Chuck Bednarik
10. Ray Nitschke
11. Derrick Thomas
12. Junior Seau
13. Chris Speilman (1989–95)
14. Ken Norton Jr.
15. Matt Millen
16. Mike Curtis
17. Thomas "Hollywood" Henderson
18. Jack Del Rio
19. Ken Harvey
20. Keena Turner

II. Linebacker Truths or Falsehoods

1. True
2. False
3. True
4. False. (Lawrence Taylor played at the University of North Carolina.)
5. True
6. True. (Buoniconti was on the 1972 Miami Dolphins' team.)
7. False. (Jordan played on one team, in Super Bowl VI.)
8. True. (Howley won the MVP as a Dallas Cowboy, playing in Super Bowl V.)

9. False. (Kevin Greene led the AFC with 14 sacks.)

10. True

11. True. (Mathews has played in 263 games.)

12. False. (Taylor led the NFL once, in 1986.)

13. True. (Tuggle has returned four fumbles for touchdowns.)

14. False. (Jack Lambert played at Kent State.)

15. True

16. False. (Greene was chosen by the Rams.)

17. True

18. True

19. False

20. False

21. False. (Lathon played for the Oilers.)

22. False. (Talley now plays for the Atlanta Falcons.)

23. True

24. True

25. False. (Lawrence Taylor has more, with 132½ sacks.)

Chapter Seven Answers

I. Pass Thieves

1. Paul Krause (81 interceptions)
2. Emlen Tunnell (79 interceptions)
3. Ken Riley (65 interceptions)
4. Ronnie Lott (63 interceptions)
5. Dave Brown (62 interceptions)
6. Emmitt Thomas (58 interceptions)
7. Johnny Robinson (57 interceptions)
8. Bobby Boyd (57 interceptions)
9. Pat Fischer (56 interceptions)
10. Lem Barney (56 interceptions)

II. Postseason Picks

1. Willie Brown. (Three interceptions and touchdowns for the Raiders in 17 postseason games.)
2. Ronnie Lott. (Two interceptions and touchdowns for the 49ers and Raiders in 20 postseason games.)
3. Lester Hayes. (Two interceptions and touchdowns for the Raiders in 13 postseason games.)
4. Darrell Green. (Two interceptions and touchdowns for the Redskins in 16 postseason games.)
5. Melvin Jenkins. (Two interceptions and touchdowns for the Seahawks and Lions in 5 postseason games.)

III. Hat Tricks

1. Ken Houston. (He returned four interceptions for the 1971 Oilers.)
2. Eric Allen. (He returned four interceptions for the 1993 Eagles.)
3. Herb Adderley. (He returned three interceptions for the 1965 Packers.)
4. Ronnie Lott. (He returned three interceptions for the 1981 49ers.)
5. Deion Sanders. (He returned three interceptions for the 1994 49ers.)

Chapter Eight Answers

I. Famous Feet

1. Pat Summerall
2. Matt Bahr
3. Lou Groza
4. Rich Karlis (against the Los Angeles Rams on November 5, 1989, in overtime)
5. Morten Andersen. (He had 22 going into the 1995 season.)
6. Jim Martin. (He kicked the field goals in 1960.)
7. Chris Boniol
8. Eddie Murray
9. Jan Stenerud
10. Tom Dempsey
11. George Blanda
12. Pat Leahy
13. Mark Moseley
14. Fuad Reveiz
15. Jim Bakken

II. Potent Punters

1. True
2. True
3. True
4. False
5. False. (Roby has had three punts blocked.)
6. True
7. False. (Guy led the league in punting three times.)
8. True
9. False. (Van Brocklin averaged 42.9 yards per punt in 523 attempts.)
10. True
11. False
12. False. (Rich Tuten led the AFC in 1995, with an average of 45.0 yards.)
13. True

14. False. (Sean Landeta led the NFC, with an average of 44.3 yards.)

15. True. (Six of his punts were blocked in 1988.)

16. False. (Sammy Baugh averaged 51.4 yards per punt in 1940.)

17. True. (This occurred from 1976 to 1983.)

18. True

19. True. (Lary led the league in punting in 1959, '61, and '65.)

20. True. (Cunningham's punt occurred in 1994.)

Chapter Nine Answers

I. Football Firsts

1. C. (Max McGee, for the 1967 Packers.)
2. A. (Bob Lilly, in the 1960 draft.)
3. A. (John Henry Johnson, in 1964.)
4. D. (Joe Namath, in 1967.)
5. C. (Sid Luckman, in 1943.)
6. B. (O. J. Simpson, in 1973.)
7. A. (Jim Benton, in 1945.)
8. B
9. A
10. C
11. D. (Mark Gastineau, in 1984.)
12. B. (Art Shell, in 1989.)
13. A
14. B. (Joe Perry, in 1953 and 1954.)
15. D. (Johnny Unitas threw for 32 touchdowns in 1959.)
16. A. (Lou Groza kicked 23 field goals in 1953.)
17. C. (Lenny Moore scored 20 touchdowns in 1964.)
18. A
19. D. (The Cleveland Browns defeated the Jets, 31–21.)
20. A. (The 1950 Rams scored 466 points.)
21. B. (Emmitt Smith played for the Dallas Cowboys, who won the Super Bowl in 1992, '93, and '95.)
22. B. (Chuck Noll's Pittsburgh Steelers won in 1975, '76, and '79.)
23. B. (Don Hutson had 105 career touchdowns.)
24. D
25. A. (Walt Kiesling, in 1942.)
26. D
27. B. (Willie Thrower played for the Chicago Bears in 1953.)
28. A. (The Steelers defeated the Vikings in 1974.)
29. B
30. A. (Bob Lilly was inducted in 1980.)
31. C. (Jack Patera coached the Seahawks in 1976.)

32. A. (Dan Marino threw a record 48 touchdown passes in 1984.)
33. C
34. C
35. A. (Miller made the Pro Bowl in 1995.)
36. B. (Don Hutson, in 1942.)
37. B. (Mark Gastineau, in 1983 and 1984.)
38. C
39. A. (The Dallas Cowboys, in Super Bowl X.)
40. C. (Weeb Ewbank won titles in 1958 and 1959 with the Colts of the NFL, and in 1968 with the Jets of the AFL.)
41. B. (The Houston Oilers, in 1968.)
42. A. (Pete Gogolak played for the Bills in 1964.)
43. B
44. B
45. A
46. B
47. C
48. B. (Jim Parker, in 1973.)
49. D. (Homer Jones, in 1965.)
50. C. (Bob Waterfield, in 1955.)

II. Record Setters

1. K. (Van Brocklin threw for 554 yards in 1951.)
2. J
3. E. (Montana completed 22 consecutive passes in 1987.)
4. I. (Dickerson rushed for 2,105 yards in 1984.)
5. H. (Marino threw for 48 touchdowns in 1984.)
6. D. (Moore led the league in scoring from 1963 to 1965.)
7. C. (Paul Hornung scored 176 points in 1960.)
8. M. (Thomas had seven sacks in one game, in 1990.)
9. A
10. L. (Gastineau had 22 sacks in 1984.)
11. N
12. P. (Hennigan had three 200-yard games in 1961.)
13. G. (Lane had 14 interceptions in 1952.)
14. R. (Allen's run occurred in Super Bowl XVIII.)

15. S
16. B
17. T. (Moore had 123 receptions in 1995.)
18. O. (Anderson's 336-yards of receptions occurred in a 1989 overtime game.)
19. F
20. Q. (Cunningham was sacked 72 times in the 1986 season.)

Chapter Ten Answers

I. NFL Head Coaches

1. True
2. False. (Sam Wyche won more than 50 games when he coached Cincinnati from 1964 to 1968.)
3. True
4. True. (Edwards coached the Redskins from 1946 to 1948.)
5. False. (The Bills were 38 and 38 under Knox.)
6. False. (Norm Van Brocklin was the first coach of the Vikings.)
7. False. (Steve Owen has the most Giant wins.)
8. True
9. True. (Seifert has compiled a record of 95–30 for a percentage of 76%.)
10. True. (Schottenheimer had a record of 75–45, for a percentage of 62.5%.)
11. False. (Marv Levy coached the Buffalo Bills to four consecutive Super Bowl appearances.)
12. False. (Parcells was drafted in the seventh round, but he chose not to play.)
13. True
14. True
15. False. (He was also the head coach of the Kansas City Chiefs.)
16. False. (Earl "Curly" Lambeau won the most games for the Packers, 212.)
17. True
18. False. (Kuharich had a record of 28–41–1.)
19. True
20. False
21. True. (Allen had a winning percentage of .681, and Ditka of .622.)
22. True
23. True
24. False

25. True
26. False. (Red Miller took the Broncos to Super Bowl XII.)
27. False. (Ewbank was inducted in 1978.)
28. True
29. False. (Ray Malavasi coached the Rams in Super Bowl XIV.)
30. False

II. Who Succeeded Whom?

1. Blanton Collier
2. Don Shula
3. Jimmy Johnson
4. Phil Bengtson
5. Paul Wiggin
6. Jim Lee Howell
7. Tom Flores
8. Les Steckel
9. Jerry Burns
10. Bill Cowher

III. Super Bowl Winning Coaches

1. Chuck Noll (4 Super Bowls)
2. Bill Walsh (3 Super Bowls)
3. Joe Gibbs (3 Super Bowls)
4. Tom Landry (2 Super Bowls)
5. Bill Parcells (2 Super Bowls)
6. Don Shula (2 Super Bowls)
7. Jimmy Johnson (2 Super Bowls)
8. Vince Lombardi (2 Super Bowls)
9. George Seifert (2 Super Bowls)
10. Tom Flores (2 Super Bowls)
11. Mike Ditka (1 Super Bowl)
12. Barry Switzer (1 Super Bowl)
13. Hank Stram (1 Super Bowl)
14. Weeb Ewbank (1 Super Bowl)
15. John Madden (1 Super Bowl)
16. Don McCafferty (1 Super Bowl)

IV. All-Time Coaching Wins

I.
1. Don Shula (328 wins)
2. George Halas (318 wins)
3. Tom Landry (250 wins)
4. Earl "Curly" Lambeau (226 wins)
5. Chuck Noll (193 wins)

II.
1. Chuck Knox (186 wins)
2. Paul Brown (166 wins)
3. Bud Grant (158 wins)
4. Steve Owen (151 wins)
5. Hank Stram (131 wins)

III.
1. Weeb Ewbank (130 wins)
2. Sid Gillman (122 wins)
3. George Allen (116 wins)
4. Mike Ditka (106 wins)
5. John Madden (103 wins)

Chapter Eleven Answers

I. NFL Champions

1. A
2. A
3. B
4. D
5. C
6. B
7. C
8. B
9. A
10. A
11. A
12. B
13. C
14. C
15. C
16. A
17. C
18. B
19. D
20. D
21. B
22. A
23. D
24. B
25. A
26. D
27. B
28. B
29. A
30. A
31. D
32. C
33. C

Chapter Twelve Answers

I. Super Bowl Chronology

1. Max McGee (for the Green Bay Packers)
2. Don Chandler
3. Matt Snell
4. Joe Kapp
5. Jim O'Brien (for the Colts)
6. Duane Thomas
7. Garo Yepremian (for the Miami Dolphins)
8. Larry Csonka
9. Dwight White
10. Lynn Swann
11. Willie Brown
12. Robert Newhouse
13. Terry Bradshaw
14. Vince Ferragamo
15. Kenny King (for the Raiders, in Super Bowl XV)
16. Dan Ross. (Jerry Rice also had 11 catches, in Super Bowl XXIII.)
17. Fulton Walker
18. Jack Squirek
19. Roger Craig
20. William Perry
21. Mark Bavaro
22. Timmy Smith
23. Stanford Jennings
24. Jerry Rice
25. Scott Norwood
26. Jim Kelly
27. Leon Lett
28. James Washington
29. Andre Coleman
30. Charles Haley

II. Going For the Ring

1. Charles Haley (5 rings)
2. Ronnie Lott (4 rings)
3. Joe Montana (4 rings)
4. Terry Bradshaw (4 rings)
5. Troy Aikman (3 rings)
6. Emmitt Smith (3 rings)
7. Ken Norton Jr. (3 rings)
8. Bart Starr (2 rings)
9. Lawrence Taylor (2 rings)
10. Jim Plunkett (2 rings)
11. Johnny Unitas (1 ring)
12. Joe Namath (1 ring)
13. Joe Theismann (1 ring)
14. Ken Stabler (1 ring)
15. Walter Payton (1 ring)

III. One-Time Winners

1. New York Jets (Super Bowl III)
2. Kansas City Chiefs (Super Bowl IV)
3. Baltimore Colts (Super Bowl V)
4. Chicago Bears (Super Bowl XX)

IV. Super Bowl MVPs

1. Bart Starr
2. Joe Namath
3. Len Dawson
4. Chuck Howley
5. Roger Staubach
6. Jake Scott
7. Larry Csonka
8. Franco Harris
9. Lynn Swann
10. Fred Biletnikoff
11. Harvey Martin and Randy White

12. Terry Bradshaw
13. Jim Plunkett
14. Joe Montana
15. John Riggins
16. Marcus Allen
17. Richard Dent
18. Phil Simms
19. Doug Williams
20. Jerry Rice
21. Ottis Anderson
22. Mark Rypien
23. Troy Aikman
24. Emmitt Smith
25. Steve Young
26. Larry Brown

Chapter Thirteen Answers

I. The AAFC

1. A
2. B
3. A
4. D
5. C
6. B
7. A
8. C
9. C
10. D

II. Did They Play in the AFL?

1. George Blanda (Oilers, 1960–66; Raiders, 1967–68)
2. Jerry Mays (Texans, 1961–62; Chiefs, 1963–69)
3. Lance Alworth (Chargers, 1962–69)
4. Bob Griese (Dolphins, 1967–69)
5. Cookie Gilchrist (Bills, 1962–64; Broncos, 1965; Dolphins, 1966; and Broncos, 1967)
6. Charlie Joiner (Oilers, 1969)
7. O. J. Simpson (Bills, 1969)
8. Bill Bergey (Bengals, 1969)
9. Larry Csonka (Dolphins, 1968–69)
10. Ken Houston (Oilers, 1967–69)

III. AFL Truths or Falsehoods

1. True
2. False. (Joe Foss was the first commissioner.)
3. False
4. True
5. True
6. True
7. False. (The Chiefs were the second team. They won Super Bowl IV.)

8. True

9. False

10. False. (Gilchrist played for the Bills, Broncos, and Dolphins.)

IV. Pick the Winner

1. Houston (24–16)
2. Houston (10–3)
3. Dallas (20–17 in overtime)
4. San Diego (51–10)
5. Buffalo (20–7)
6. Buffalo (23–0)
7. Kansas City (31–7)
8. Oakland (40–7)
9. New York (27–23)
10. Kansas City (17–7)

Chapter Fourteen Answers

I. The Hall of Fame

1. Wayne Millner
2. Lenny Moore
3. Mike Ditka
4. Jim Brown
5. Mel Blount
6. Sammy Baugh
7. Joe Namath
8. Alan Page
9. Paul Warfield
10. Randy White
11. Charley Taylor
12. Norm Van Brocklin
13. Larry Wilson
14. Jack Lambert
15. Gino Marchetti
16. Ray Nitschke
17. Johnny Unitas
18. George Connor
19. Sid Luckman
20. Sam Huff

II. Can You Pick Out the Hall of Famers?

1. Charley Taylor
2. Fred Biletnikoff
3. Bob Griese
4. Larry Csonka
5. Herb Adderley
6. Frank Gifford
7. Otto Graham
8. Art Shell
9. Len Dawson
10. Lee Roy Selmon
11. Chuck Bednarik
12. Jim Parker
13. Joe Greene
14. Emlen Tunnell
15. O. J. Simpson
16. Jim Langer
17. Don Maynard
18. Alan Page
19. Jim Marshall
20. Steve Largent
21. Raymond Berry
22. Doak Walker
23. Willie Wood
24. Jan Stenerud
25. Jackie Smith

Chapter Fifteen Answers

I. Draft Choices

1. Atlanta Falcons
2. Tampa Bay Buccaneers
3. Baltimore Colts
4. Indianapolis Colts
5. Tampa Bay Buccaneers
6. New England Patriots
7. Los Angeles Rams
8. Cleveland Browns
9. Baltimore Colts
10. Cleveland Browns
11. Atlanta Falcons
12. Chicago Bears
13. Los Angeles Rams
14. Indianapolis Colts
15. Los Angeles Raiders
16. New Orleans Saints
17. New Orleans Saints
18. New York Giants
19. New York Jets
20. Pittsburgh Steelers
21. St. Louis Cardinals
22. New York Giants
23. Washington Redskins
24. Indianapolis Colts
25. Houston Oilers

II. Players and Their Birthplaces

1. J	7. A	13. H	19. C	25. E
2. L	8. P	14. R	20. N	
3. K	9. G	15. V	21. Y	
4. F	10. D	16. Q	22. W	
5. O	11. M	17. S	23. I	
6. B	12. X	18. T	24. U	

III. Matching Names

1. Willie Anderson
2. John Elliot
3. Billy Johnson
4. Steve McMichael
5. Ray Hamilton
6. Thomas Henderson
7. Gerald McNeil
8. William Perry
9. Walter Payton
10. Jack Tatum
11. Johnny Jones
12. Raghib Ismail
13. Lance Alworth
14. Fred Williamson
15. Sam Cunningham
16. John Fuqua
17. Ted Hendricks
18. Craig Heyward
19. Gary Johnson
20. Joe Greene
21. Paul Hornung
22. Eddie Payton
23. John Matuszak
24. Elroy Hirsch
25. Skip Thomas
26. Dennis Winston
27. Pat Fischer
28. Ken Stabler
29. Deion Sanders
30. Roger Staubach

IV. Team Nicknames

1. C
2. D
3. G
4. E
5. J
6. I
7. H
8. B
9. A
10. F

V. Stadiums

1. F
2. D
3. H
4. I
5. J
6. M
7. N
8. C
9. B
10. A
11. O
12. G
13. E
14. L
15. K

VI. Past and Present Truths or Falsehoods

1. True
2. True
3. True
4. False
5. False. (Walker beat out Lujack, 128–129.)
6. True
7. True
8. False. (Walker played at Southern Methodist University.)
9. True
10. False. (Trippi played for the Chicago Cardinals.)
11. True
12. False. (Wood competed in two, Super Bowls I and II.)
13. False. (They lost the 1960 NFL title game to the Eagles.)
14. True
15. True
16. False
17. True
18. False. (Earl Morrall started at quarterback.)
19. False
20. False
21. True
22. True
23. False. (Taylor had a league-high 1,474 yards.)
24. False. (The Oakland Raiders beat the Dolphins.)
25. True
26. True
27. False. (Super Bowl IX was played at Tulane Stadium.)
28. False. (Don Coryell, with a record of 42–29–1, is the Cardinals' all-time winningest coach.)
29. False. (Sammy Baugh led the league in passing six times: 1937, '40, '43, '45, '47 and '49.)
30. False. (Jim Brown won a record rushing titles.)
31. False. (Dorsett played for Dallas in Super Bowl XII, which Dallas won over Denver, 27–10.)
32. False. (Eric Dickerson rushed for over 2,000 yards in 1984, and O. J. Simpson for over 2,000 in 1973.)

33. True
34. True. (Gibbs had three Super Bowl wins, and Landry two.)
35. False. (The Jets appeared in one, Super Bowl III.)
36. True. (Walls led the league in interceptions in 1981, '82, and '85.)
37. False. (Steve Young has the highest career pass rating, with 96.8.)
38. True. (Bledsoe threw 70 passes in a 1994 game against Minnesota.)
39. True
40. False. (The Raiders won three: Super Bowls XI, XV, and XVIII.)
41. False. (John Madden is the Raiders' winningest coach.)
42. False. (Stabler threw 150 touchdown passes.)
43. True
44. True
45. False. (Chuck Noll won Super Bowls IX, X, XIII, and XIV.)
46. True. (Young set the record in 1994.)
47. True
48. True. (Karlis, who kicked seven in 1989, shares the record with Jim Bakken, who kicked seven in 1967.)
49. False. (Christian Okoye, with 4,897 yards in 1987–92, is the Chiefs' all-time rushing leader.)
50. False. (Bill Kenney, with 4,348 yards in 1983, holds the record.)

VII. Retired Numbers

1. D	6. H	11. M	16. T
2. G	7. B	12. S	17. P
3. J	8. E	13. K	18. Q
4. A	9. F	14. C	19. L
5. I	10. O	15. R	20. N

Index

126

ABOUT THE AUTHORS

Dom Forker is a 1961 graduate of Mount Saint Mary's College in Emmitsburg, Maryland. Over the past 35 years, he has coordinated careers in both teaching and writing. He has written 17 books on sports, most notably *The Men of Autumn* and *Sweet Seasons* (which are histories of the 1949–64 New York Yankees, who won 14 pennants and 9 World Series in 16 years), and *Baseball Brain Teasers, Big League Baseball Puzzlers,* and *Test Your Baseball IQ,* a series of three books that deal with baseball rules.

Ted Forker is a 1992 graduate of the University of Dayton. He is pursuing a writing and sports management career. *Pro Football Brain Teasers* is the 26-year-old's first book.